MECHANICS' INSTITUTE
~ MECHANICS' ~
MERCANTILE LIBRARY

On Time and
On Budget

On Time
and
On Budget

A Home Renovation Survival Guide

John Rusk

DOUBLEDAY

New York   London   Toronto   Sydney   Auckland

PUBLISHED BY DOUBLEDAY
a division of Bantam Doubleday Dell Publishing Group, Inc.
1540 Broadway, New York, New York 10036

DOUBLEDAY and the portrayal of an anchor with a dolphin are trademarks of
Doubleday, a division of Bantam Doubleday Dell Publishing Group, Inc.

Book design by Richard Oriolo

Library of Congress Cataloging-in-Publication Data

Rusk, John.
On time and on budget: a home renovation survival guide / John Rusk.
p.   cm.
1. Dwellings—Remodeling—Planning.   I. Title
TH4816.R85   1996
643′.7—dc20   95-44737
CIP

ISBN 0-385-47501-2
Printed in the United States of America
June 1996
First Edition
1   2   3   4   5   6   7   8   9   10

For Mary

Contents

Part Three: Beginning Construction

Part Four: Ending Construction

On Time and On Budget

Introduction:
The Basics

Every year, hundreds of thousands of families find themselves in the middle of an ugly home renovation. They first try to do it themselves according to television shows and do-it-yourself books. Failing that, they hire a contractor and maybe an architect who paints a beautiful picture, takes their deposit, and then plunges them into a nightmare. These families watch as their belongings are destroyed, their savings are decimated by extras, and their jobs jeopardized by having to take off work to meet contractors who are habitually late. Finally, their project has taken so long and their life and marriage are in such shambles that they fire their contractor and hire someone who is twice as expensive but who limps them along to the completion of something they never would have chosen.

At the same time, other home renovation projects go well. The owners start early and have a pleasant design period where they work out, with an architect or designer, what it is they like and need and come up with a complete, beautiful design. They find a good contractor who takes a hard look at their drawings and makes suggestions for building it more efficiently without sacrificing its integrity. The contractor goes on to build the job, and despite the inevitable problems, the architect, contractor, and owner work through them and they end up finishing the job on time and on budget. The final project might look like the pictures in the "home" magazines or maybe they just function well and look nice.

How do we get to that magazine kitchen? How do we create a design that not only looks good but suits the style of a particular family, that has a nook to pay bills and room for guests to sit and chat?

How also do we make the process enjoyable? How do we stop the endless bickering between contractors, architects, and owners? How do we ensure that at the end of the project, everyone has something to be proud of and that it was done on time and on budget?

These concerns are the subject of this book.

I'm a successful contractor in New York City and I've built quite a few of those magazine kitchens, bathrooms, and living rooms. I've worked with some demanding people and I've delivered some amazing work. Most of my clients got more than they ever dreamed, the architects got some wonderful photographs for their portfolio, and I made a profit; but over the years, I began to wonder why sometimes the jobs didn't go smoothly, why sometimes my performance was less than I had wished it to be.

While I pondered this, I had also noticed that my clients, high-powered lawyers and corporate heads, were consistently besting me at the negotiation table. They skillfully used their power to push me into accepting terms that were less than adequate for me and usually resulted in a job that went badly. At the same time, some kindhearted clients were also partnering up with me for ordeals. Hearing my plight, my brother-in-law, who's a negotiator for the state of New Jersey, gave me *Getting to Yes,* by Roger Fisher and William Ury

(Penguin, 1982). This seminal negotiation text is the heart of the Program on Negotiation at Harvard Law School. It opened the door for me to modern negotiation theory, which held the key to resolving my problems. The basic theory of the book is that rather than each of two parties choosing a position and then having a knockout fight to see who wins, a better agreement can be fashioned by examining the specific needs of each party and designing a creative agreement that satisfies both sides. In this way, no one loses, and often, in the exploration, people find themselves a better deal than they were originally asking for.

Intrigued by this idea, I began practicing the book's concepts on my own business and found myself on a more equal playing field with my powerful clients. And I would later find that educating less sophisticated clients in these principles also produced better renovations. Exhausting the bookstore's negotiation titles, I finally enrolled in the Program on Negotiation at Harvard and began commuting to Boston. I had planned to study pure negotiation, but my instructor, Bruce Stedman, suggested I study the construction industry and apply negotiation principles to it. The program's instructors had mostly been concentrating on environmental and international negotiations, but they were very interested in the "micro" problems of the home renovation and construction industry. After a semester of study, I reported the following:

- Negotiation in the home construction and renovation industry is very ineffective. Rather than finding solutions that are the most profitable for everyone by using everyone's resources to the best advantage, negotiation for home renovation and construction mostly relies on a set of unspoken rules about how business is conducted that leaves the contractor almost entirely out of the planning phase and the owner out of the construction phase.

- Because many of the industry's rules have been developed by architects, the client is often not fully involved with the project. Traditionally, the client provides direction and money to the architect, who then acts as their representative. Contractors are kept at arm's length in an adversarial role against the client-architect team. The architect, then, is positioned as the expert. I believe that these assumptions create an uncooperative working relationship that doesn't fully exploit the abilities of the players.

- At the same time, I realized that by applying solid negotiation principles, this adversarial relationship could be transformed. Rather than leaving the unfortunate architect to shoulder all the intellectual burden and communication between parties, I saw that in fact the client and the contractor were better suited to certain tasks, leaving the architect free to concentrate on design and function. I saw we could restructure the equation from an "everyone for himself or herself" model to a "unified team striving to overcome a mutual problem" model. Suddenly, I realized that the process of renovation could be rewarding for everyone involved. This reminded me of those projects that had been successful for me, for they had shared this quality of teamwork: client, architect, and contractor working together to solve the challenges inherent in construction.

- As I thought more deeply about how to infuse every renovation project with the spirit of teamwork, I realized who the key was. Not the architect, who would still be responsible for turning the aesthetics, needs, time limitations, and budget of the client into a concrete plan; and not the contractor, who would continue to be responsible for executing this plan beautifully, on schedule and budget. The key to a successful renovation project is the client.

Rather than standing limply on the sidelines doing little more than writing checks, the client must become the *producer* of his or her project. Just like a movie producer, the homeowner must choose the talent, determine a budget, and work with the architect to develop a style. The homeowner must make it possible for a wide variety of artists to perform their best work.

The owner need not spend time learning the proper way to plumb a sink, frame an addition, or design a kitchen—jobs for which there are already fully capable professionals who will deliver a better job than homeowners can ever do themselves. But owners can properly arrange and control the renovation; and their strong leadership will provide a better project for architects and contractors alike.

Setting a budget and defining taste are the first essential steps to a rewarding and successful construction project, and they are steps that homeowners must take themselves. Budget and taste are the rudder and ballast of any job, steering all the players through the process as clearly as a movie producer who proposes making a comedy for $10 million to be released next year. Given that information at the start, architects and contractors will know what to do. It seems simple, but so many times I've been asked to bid something by people who claim that they don't really know how much money they want to spend or what kind of things they like. Classic? Contemporary? Mediterranean? Without this basic homework done, the reputable industry professionals are going to be turned off, and the owner is going to be left with people eager to exploit their uncertainties.

Basic start-up tasks such as hiring the architect are obviously done by the homeowners. How should they prepare? They must understand the difference between an architect and a designer and an engineer. They must have a method to find good talent that concurrently provides them with power in the relationship beyond money. They need to know exactly how to structure their relationship with a design professional so that they can get that designer's best work.

One of the Program on Negotiation's rules was that for any solution to work efficiently, it must be good for everyone. Otherwise, someone is going to have to enforce it and someone else is going to be constantly trying to get around it. I have looked diligently for solutions to the problems of the construction industry that serve the needs of not only the client but the contractor and the design professional as well. Essentially, I have renegotiated the rules of the construction industry by discussing my ideas with other contractors, architects, and owners to find out what they would agree to if the result was a better, more profitable way of doing business. Many people were eager to help and make contributions and criticisms because they all know that the system as it exists continually fails. What I have been most surprised by was the willingness of my current clients to go along with some radical changes to the way business has been done in the past. You'll find these as you progress through this book.

But how does the client learn this role? I don't believe it's possible to list sixty quick suggestions "magazine style" and watch the client suddenly be transformed into a master construction facilitator.

What is essential is that the owner acquire an in-depth knowledge of how construction and renovation jobs progress. How do the nightmares happen? How do the dream projects happen? And not just from the point of view of the client but from the points of view of the architect and contractor as well. We'll then analyze these problems and opportunities and make specific suggestions for strategies and tactics that will solve the headaches and capitalize on the opportunities.

My book is broken into four parts, which are the four parts of any renovation or construction: Design, Contracting, Beginning Construction, and Ending Construction. Each part is a self-contained unit, covering all of the problems and solutions for that part of the project. Though you can read the whole book at once, it has been designed to be read over four separate time periods. Read the design section and then embark on that part of your project using the understanding and strategies while they are fresh in your head. As you reach the end of the design phase of your project, you'll want to read the contracting section to prepare you for the next phase of your real-life work, and so on. It is my desire that you use the whole book, and reading it in shorter sections should make that task more manageable.

We'll start each of these sections with the story of Larry and

Cindy Hampton, who serve as our bad examples. We'll analyze their problems by looking at the five areas of conflict: money, time, management, power, and quality. We'll look at these issues from the points of view of the contractor, homeowner, and architect.

This understanding of all sides of the issues will make clear why my suggestions not only are useful but make sense for all three parties involved.

I'll conclude each section with the story of a very good renovation project. We'll watch how Tom and Michelle Finley use these specific suggestions to make their renovation a success, though initially they were faced with many of the same problems as the Hamptons.

Within each of the four parts, I'll also have a unique topic specific to that period of the job.

During Design I'll refer you to the appendix for advice about materials.

During Contracting I'll refer you to the appendix for a discussion of negotiation theory as taught by the Program on Negotiation at Harvard and best expressed in *Getting to Yes*. The appendices include a section that examines various contracts and provides sample wording necessary to implement the suggestions of this book; also included is a sample change order.

During Beginning Construction I'll refer you to the appendix for a thorough examination of communication among architect, contractor, and client. We'll go through ways to improve it by relying on graphic representation of problems, establishing quick lines of communication, and planning for weekly meetings that cover everything from paint colors to change orders.

During Ending Construction you can refer to the appendix to review the various methods of dispute resolution, from litigation to arbitration and mediation, as well as the brand of dispute avoidance that this book has at its core.

By the end of the book, you will know how to:

- Set a budget range

- Hire an architect

- Make sure the project reflects and satisfies your taste and needs

- Use a contractor as a consultant to lower the bid

- Choose materials with high performance and low maintenance

- Develop and exert power over the architect and contractor without annoying either of them

- Improve the communication of the job

- Make your project a "jewel" in the eyes of the architect and contractor so that they will want to use it for future references

- Handle disputes

Most important, you will learn how to achieve the goals of the architect and contractor as well as your own. You will learn how to build a beautiful project, on time and on budget.

A note on style: The contractor will be "he," since contractors, by and large, are male. To balance things out and to honor the many qualified female architects and designers I've worked with, I'll refer to both the good and bad design professionals as "she."

Part One

Design

1

The Hamptons— Laying the Groundwork for a Nightmare Kitchen

Larry Hampton threw the Pathfinder into reverse and whined backward past the back door and around in front of the house to wait for his wife. Cindy didn't like to use the back door. Her mother had been part of the moneyless rich, people whose fortunes have long since been spent, but who hold on to ancient social mores as if they could supplant a bank account.

Larry liked the rules, but only because they were better than the intuitive sludge of his parents' poverty. He watched the front door of the house, hoping that Cindy would be in a good mood when she came out. For the past three years they'd been trying to decide what to do with their kitchen. Then just last week Cindy heard about a place she had to see—but wouldn't say why. She said they could just go to this place and buy the whole kitchen.

Larry tooted the horn. She was in there, dressing or writing notes or moving a vase around; part of the whole thing with her mother. When Larry had first started going out with Cindy, he found it exotic—the waiting in a den for Cindy to come down. When she did, she was always completely put together, made up, and truly beautiful.

"Come on," he mumbled to the dashboard of the Nissan.

Larry's mood started to change as he looked at his house. As far as he was concerned, a new kitchen was just a way of keeping up with the neighbors. Fixing it up wasn't going to make the food taste better. It wasn't going to make the food any more economical to prepare. They had some money in the bank, but with bills coming in, Larry really didn't know how much he could spend. He wished she'd come out.

Cindy looked out through the front window at Larry hunched over the steering wheel of the Pathfinder. His bright blue and yellow down coat made him look like some kind of vending machine filler. The vending machine filler and his wife. Mrs. Vending Machine Filler. No matter how pulled together she looked, that down coat made her Mrs. Vending Machine Filler. Cindy didn't see why Larry dressed like this when he went out with her. It was as if he was saying mea culpa for having money in the bank. It annoyed her.

Down the block, she could see the edge of Tim and Janice's house. Janice Conroy had kept the ladies of the neighborhood spellbound with tales of their renovation. The whole summer, Janice complained about the work crews, the extras, the dust, and the idiot architect while everyone listened. Cindy didn't dare bring up their own plans, because that was all they were. Plans. Plans with the vending machine filler.

Cindy left the window and walked back into the kitchen to get her wish list. Their kitchen had been remodeled in the seventies by the former owners of the house. It was worked in a Tudor theme with dark-stained wood nailed over white (now yellowed) walls with gold plastic translucent windows between the kitchen and dining room. Pizza restaurants had subsequently taken over the theme.

Cindy didn't like themes. Janice's theme was brass and green.

Cindy was sure she'd seen it in some bar. It was all Cindy could do to stop from bursting out laughing when she saw the pool table shade hanging over the eat-in kitchen table. That light was Janice's husband, Tim. Larry was bad but not as bad as Tim. Besides, Cindy wouldn't allow anything like that.

One of Cindy's old friends was an interior decorator and Cindy had been urging Larry to hire her. Larry's retort—that he had married his wife for her good taste—was a flattering point, but she guessed he just didn't want to spend the money on a professional designer. Still, she did know enough not to make her kitchen look like a bowling alley.

So now she was going to get her kitchen and make Larry happy, too. She had found out about a lumberyard that had "closeout" kitchens. Apparently, they had a lot of junk, but every once in a while you could find a real bargain because the owner didn't know what he had. This excited Cindy.

She snapped her purse shut, checked her lipstick, and swung wide the front door.

The oak floor at Jack's lumberyard was worn into deep valleys in front of the counters. Jack himself lived in a beautifully restored twenties mansion, but he liked to keep the lumberyard looking like a place where a man could find a bargain. Jack worked from seven to five every day, watched the till, and sold whatever he could to make a dollar. Jack believed in selling cheap. His father, the first Jack, taught him that price brought customers. No better way.

As Jack grew up, he watched some of his friends take over their parents' business, and he learned from their hubris. Many of these misguided souls were embarrassed by the bargain nature of the ragtag shops and tried to dress things up. Their customers stopped coming and things went downhill.

Jack loved his worn-through shop floor and he knew that every person, poor or rich, who crossed his doors loved it, too. It felt like a bargain.

Jack specialized in closeouts. What another man was happy to get rid of, Jack was happy to sell as his stock-in-trade. He bought discontinued kitchen displays from other lumberyards for little more than the cost of dismantling them. The other lumberyards imagined themselves too high-class to sell discontinued kitchen cabinets, since no house conforms to the shape of a lumberyard display, and without the cabinets still in production, filling in the missing pieces becomes impossible. That didn't matter to Jack.

Jack advertised his low prices on kitchens, and when people streamed in to buy them, he had an uncanny ability to size up their fantasies and present his product as their low-priced answer. Some needed to believe that Jack was an idiot who had made a grave error when he priced a particular kitchen. Others wanted to believe that fate and good deeds had brought them to this strange moment in time when prices were artificially low and goods were exactly suited to them. Still others, though, needed to know the truth—that these were discontinued cabinets and they were idiots to buy them.

Jack had a big window on his parking lot and he kept it clear of merchandise so he could see the cars his customers drove. Now he watched as the Pathfinder pulled up.

As Jack saw it, a Pathfinder was a cheap knockoff of a Range Rover. It was an expensive vehicle, so the owners had money, but they liked their money to look like more than they had.

The wife was wearing an expensive scarf, very clean. Put together. He was wearing a truck driver down coat. Jack figured they had a "traditional marriage" where they hated each other: The husband wanted to go to a ballgame with the boys and complain about the wife; she wanted to get out with the girls, dish the neighbors, and bitch about the husband. She had probably wanted the Range Rover. He was cheap.

Jack imagined this was what hunters felt when first seeing a ten-point buck.

Jack didn't believe in bringing consumers straight to the kitchen that was right for them. First, he showed them the "Tudor Style" kitchen, then the chipped Formica one. He got them so disgusted that by the time he brought them to something even moderately nice, it was like a cold drink on a hot day. Nearly irresistible.

The pink Formica model with the broken doors always made them squirm. "Here's a kitchen that we sell a lot of. It's fairly attractive, should last for ten years, and it has a great price. You could get someone to install this in a day."

Jack was enjoying the expression on both Larry's and Cindy's faces. Larry looked like he was ready to reach in his back pocket and start throwing him money, but Cindy looked like she was going to have a nervous breakdown and run screaming from the store. Jack wanted to drive her a little further before he found her "the right thing." He knew just what it was. He continued, "You know where we sell a lot of these?"

"No, where?" Larry asked gullibly.

"The valley. We sell tons of these down there in the valley where they have all those developments."

"Larry, let's go." Cindy had reached her breaking point.

"You don't like this kitchen?" Jack asked.

"It's not for us. Larry, let's go."

"You don't have anything else?" Larry said. He knew when he was in a place where bargains could be found.

Jack scratched his head. "Boy. You don't like this kitchen. You didn't like the other one I showed you—the Tudor one." Suddenly Jack perked up, then reversed and muttered, "No," under his breath.

"What?" Larry said.

"Ah, I already sold it. I'm sorry, I don't have anything else. Thanks for stopping by." Jack started to walk them to the door.

"What is it that you sold?" Cindy asked.

"A traditional kitchen, molding, solid wood, glass doors. That's probably more what you're looking for?"

"Maybe," Cindy said warily. "But you've already sold it?"

"Well"—Jack bobbed his head back and forth—"just about. They went home to check measurements."

"So you haven't sold it," Cindy said.

"They're from Rosedale. I don't want to mess with people from

Rosedale. They'd probably send their lawyer." Jack made a hint at a laugh and then said, "You're probably from Rosedale. I'm sorry."

Larry stepped in now. "Let's just take a look before we go. Maybe it will give us an idea."

"I really shouldn't," Jack said.

"Please," Cindy said, and she turned on her best smile.

Jack looked around. "All right, come on back. But it's just to take a look."

He turned and walked quickly back through the store, not allowing himself a glance at them but knowing the looks they were exchanging between themselves.

Jack brought them to his best kitchen. "You can see why people around here don't go for it. It's classical. Not fancy. It has real crown molding instead of that fake plastic stuff. People around here just can't appreciate that."

Larry said "This is a closeout?"

"Well, this is the price," Jack said, raising the sticker. It read "$3900.00."

"That's why you haven't sold any of these," Cindy said. "That price is ridiculous. Half of this price I could believe."

Jack looked stunned. "Half?" Then he smiled. "Well, you've got your idea. I really need to get back."

"Listen, let's not get riled up," Larry broke in. "My wife is just suggesting, and I think it's fair, that closeout prices are typically much lower."

"I never give anything more than ten percent off in the store. Even in a closeout."

The "Pathfinders" just looked at him. Jack looked back and shook his head. "This is beside the point anyway. I have these people coming back for them."

Cindy looked at the cabinets very carefully. "What were you charging the couple from Rosedale?"

"We hadn't really settled on a price yet." Jack left a hole wide enough to drive a truck through.

And in Cindy came. "Then what you're talking about is theoretical. We're interested in buying cabinets today. Walking right out of here with them. Now, if we were going to buy right now—no going home and checking measurements—how much would you charge us? I'm thinking about half this price."

Jack sighed. "Listen, I can't sell these cabinets for half off. I've got more than that in them. Go home, think it over, come back in a few days. I'm always getting something new in."

"Make us an offer, then."

Jack looked at the cabinets. He had bought them for $400 a week and a half ago. "I guess I could give them to you for twenty percent off if you bought them today. That's what, I guess three thousand dollars?"

The Hamptons looked at each other. "That's not very much," Cindy said. "I think we're going to have to go home and think about this."

"That's fine. It's actually what I was hoping. If the people from Rosedale decide they don't want them, then maybe I could come down a little."

Cindy and Larry were in anguish.

"Give us a minute, would you?" Larry asked.

"Take all the time in the world."

Jack wandered off and wrote up the bill for $2,925. Which was 25 percent off. It wasn't a bad morning.

"Excuse me, Jack." Larry had the look of concern on his face. "Listen, Jack, we asked for fifty percent off originally, we'll come down to thirty and that's it."

Jack shook his head. "That's fine. Listen, come back tomorrow. If they're still here, we can talk."

"Twenty-five off, then, and we'll take them right now."

Jack picked up the sticker price. "Eehhh. Then you tell me what to say to the people from Rosedale."

Cindy smiled. "Tell them we apologize."

Larry and Cindy watched as Frank walked around the kitchen, the cabinets stacked in the dining room just beyond them. They'd found Frank through a small ad in the yellow pages that repeated "inexpensive" three different ways. He was a big man, the kind who was probably buying beer for his friends at an early age.

"Did the lumberyard give you any kind of sketch of what you have here?"

"No, they were closeouts. What we need you to do is come up with a plan and then give us a price."

"Did you have any idea of how you wanted them to go?"

"No. We'll need you to figure that out. I think we'll want the island somewhere here with the sink in it and the oven over there. Or maybe the island with the rangetop in it."

Frank looked at the kitchen. His head was swimming. Without a plan he had no idea what to do, but he knew if he told them to hire an architect, the architect would want to bring in her own contractors, and Frank wasn't on a friendly basis with any architects anymore.

"Okay," Frank said. "We'll just have to improvise. When do you want me to start?"

"We'll need a price first."

"Well, without a plan, it's kind of hard to know what the price is. I think we start and then work it out."

Cindy tensed up. "Larry, could I speak to you for a minute? Excuse us, Frank."

Cindy took Larry out into the hallway. "I was afraid of this, Larry. I think he just wants to get us in the position where our kitchen is all taken apart and then he gives us a bill."

Larry looked at her—she really must believe he was an idiot. "Cindy, I'm not going to let anyone start without a firm price. If he won't give us a price, then we'll find some other contractors. The newspapers are full of them."

Larry and Cindy went back into the kitchen. "Listen, Frank," Larry said, "if you can't give us some idea of the price, we're going to have to get some other people in here who can. It's a simple job. Remove the existing cabinets, install the new cabinets. There will be an island with either the sink in it or the stove. I don't see that there will be much difference either way. You'll still have to hook them both up."

"You're right," Frank said, "it's just a matter of hooking them up. I would say the price to remove your old stuff and install the new is about two thousand dollars."

Cindy exploded. *"Two thousand?* We're paying for the cabinets. What are your materials? Two thousand dollars' worth of screws? We probably have some screws in the garage you could use. That's ridiculous. We'll call someone else."

"Ma'am, it's just an approximation. I might be way off."

"You *are* way off. We'll get back to you."

Cindy was sitting in the kitchen looking out to the driveway, waiting for Karen. Karen was her friend, the interior designer that Larry had done everything he possibly could to offend and keep out of this project. Larry resented having to pay someone to do something that was completely superfluous. To him, it was the equivalent of having friends over to get their advice, except that this friend charged $750 to do it. Cindy had only prevailed after first getting Karen to agree to do some basic plans for $500 and then after she and Larry had gone through the dizzying experience of interviewing three more contractors from the newspaper.

The first, Prime Construction, took a look at the pile of cabinets, measured the wall, and then drew up a plan that included a new floor, moving one of the walls, and new wallpaper. He called back two days later: $7,000.

The second contractor they played telephone tag with. He missed the first appointment completely. For the second, he at least called to say he'd be late. Two hours later, he showed up, took a look at the kitchen, spoke quite convincingly of what a great job he could do, left without measurements, and never called again or returned their call.

The third contractor was the queerest bird. His name was Giovanni DeTomaso. He suggested that they had better hire an architect and draw up a set of plans. In addition he suggested that they hire him to work with the architect to explore what was inside the wall they were thinking about removing so they wouldn't have any surprises once they started. He also wanted to be paid to figure various cost options. Larry and Cindy thought that paying for what every contractor is supposed to do for free was ludicrous and they sent him packing.

After two weeks of having their dining room filled with cabinets, they had two numbers. Frank's $2,000 and Prime Construction's $7,000.

Cindy laughed a little as she watched for Karen's car. At least now she had something to bitch about to her friends. That was how Karen got involved. Karen heard the story, then convinced her that the only way they would be able to get reasonable prices and compare apples to apples was to have a set of plans drawn up.

Karen's Buick pulled up and Cindy took a quick look at the dining room. It was a mess. The cabinets stood there; some were dirty, one already had a nick out of the corner—a result of Larry Jr.'s hockey stick. Imagining what Karen was about to see, Cindy realized how tawdry the whole place looked. Karen would talk behind her back.

She flipped on the porch light and called for Larry.

Karen looked great and had a cardboard tube under her arm. "I'm really excited about these plans," Karen said as she plopped them down on the table. "There's an island in the center with range and a hood, the sink's by the window so you can watch the yard while you're doing the dishes. It's more modern. Crisp."

Cindy glanced over at Larry. The plans did look great. She'd even drawn some red peppers on the grill. It was just what she'd always wanted.

"Karen," Larry said, "you know, there seem to be more cabinets here than what we have, and it looks like these are drawn differently from what we have."

"Larry, if you want a nice kitchen, if you're going to spend the money and go through the time and the expense, you're going to have to throw out those cabinets in the dining room and start over."

Larry looked at the plans. "If you think I'm paying you five hundred dollars to tell me that, when we specifically told you to figure out how we were going to fit those cabinets into this kitchen, you're crazy."

"They don't fit. Those cabinets do not fit into this kitchen. I called Jack's Lumber and they are discontinued. He says he told you that. Since I learned that these cabinets are of no use to you, I thought I'd spend my time constructively and come up with a decent plan for your kitchen."

Larry stood without a word and walked off down the hallway, leaving Karen and Cindy looking at the renderings, at how the center island hood was swallowing the steam from the peppers.

2

Money Problems

There are always money problems. Either there's not enough money or there is enough but along with it comes such psychological pressure to hold on to it that there might as well not be any. Ironically, it's often this pressure that built the surplus money in the first place.

Money is the heart of almost every problem in construction, and for this reason it is the heart of this book. People have a great fear of being taken advantage of, and as a result, they often work hard to protect themselves. Many times they inadvertently end up robbing themselves by their actions more effectively than a thief ever could.

Dishonest contractors, owners, and architects certainly exist, and I'll show you some simple ways to detect them. But the more important work of this book is learning how to work with the honest, well-meaning contractors and architects who can still rob you blind. Not because they want to, but because you end up spending more money than you should for something that you don't want and that will have little resale value.

Typically, most owners have spent five years saving the money they are about to spend in three months on a contractor. This slightly dusty contractor is about to receive every skipped vacation, every postponed new car, every nice lunch avoided. The very least that the owners expect for this tremendous outpouring of their own cash is a heartfelt thanks from the contractor.

Instead, the contractor often has his own money problems. He is busy worrying about the notices for withholding taxes and insurance premiums, about getting paid for the extras that have mounted from the owners changing their mind, and about his wife's anger at having spent their savings to finish a client's job—a job that may not make them one red cent of profit. The least the contractor could expect for this herculean effort is a heartfelt thanks from the architect.

But the architect has her own problems. She can't believe she has given the client a price to do a simple job—and ended up designing ten different plans, being blamed by the contractor for his inefficiencies, has $20,000 worth of student loans left, has been yelled at by the client at least a dozen times (usually at ten-thirty at night), and all of this for a salary less than a letter carrier.

Being a letter carrier is a tough job, but it doesn't require a master's degree and you're usually finished at three.

Each of these people has serious money problems that are very closely linked to their psychological well-being. Let's examine each a bit more closely.

Contractors can be split into two money-based groups: high-end contractors and lowball contractors. High-end contractors charge top dollar for their work and work hard to justify the extra expense. They work in every budget level, from thousand-dollar desks to million-dollar dialysis units—but their bids will always be at least 15 percent higher than their lowball brothers. The misconception, though, is that high-end contractors charge what they do because the market will bear it.

The truth is, the high-end contractor has higher costs. Rather than paying semiskilled carpenters $80 a day, the high-end contractor will pay $110. Rather than electricians who charge $80 per outlet, he may employ electricians who charge $150 per outlet. The difference is often subtle. Imagine a two-foot-wide Sheetrock column in your house that you want a sconce centered on. Unbeknownst to you, there is a stud directly in the middle of that column. When the $80-an-outlet electrician cuts his hole, he's going to run into that stud and he will then probably install the light an inch and a half off center. The $150-an-outlet electrician may spend an extra fifteen minutes cutting out a stud because it drives him crazy to have things off center.

As a first rule, if you don't mind things off center and bumpy, you can hire a lowball contractor. If those things bother you, hire the man who pays his electrician well.

The lowball contractor gets his work by charging the lowest possible prices and concentrating on volume. In order to make his profit back, he economizes in every way possible, from cheaper labor to using off-brand materials to skimping on the insulation.

Either one of these contractors can be an honest man. Either one can make good money at his work. Whether he makes money or not is related more to management practices and we'll talk about that later.

Contractors often have money problems and the reason is simple: They build one-of-a-kind projects and have no full idea of what these will cost to make. This is bad enough, but they are often bidding against someone who has even less of an idea of what the project should cost. Or they are competing with someone who is intentionally underbidding in order to get the job and who then plans to compensate for the low bid by charging for lots of extras once construction begins.

Clients usually see nothing wrong with the underbidding contractor (usually because they don't want to), so contractors faced with an underbidding contractor often have to choose between losing the job and lowering their price, hoping they can make the money back by working faster. Failing that, they'll have to borrow money from the next job to finish the first job. This round-robin can accumulate, particularly when the IRS enters in. Typically, contractors must make monthly and quarterly installment payments for their taxes, but no government agent comes to the house to pick it up, so if the date slips past, nothing bad happens—immediately.

Imagine the contractor who is deep in the middle of a job that he has underbid. He's out of money to pay the plumber, who's threatened to walk off this job and go on to the next if he doesn't get his check immediately. Our contractor then gets the down payment check for his next job that starts in two weeks. He pays the plumber out of this money (it's in his same general business bank account). Then our contractor gets a threatening notice from the IRS that he hasn't paid his quarterly withholding from two quarters ago and that if he doesn't pay it now, they are going to seize his assets—his tools. Our contractor pays the IRS out of that down payment check, too.

Peace reigns.

Until the next job starts in two weeks.

The architect or designer lives a curious irony. Since her main clients are wealthy, she herself has to appear wealthy so that it is acceptable that she is giving them advice about how to live. The problem is that architecture pays its practitioners half to a quarter of the wages of many of their clients. The average salary for an architect with her own practice is around $43,100, but this figure includes the much higher income of architects with well-established commercial practices. The architects who are likely to be available for small renovations are going to have a lower salary; perhaps closer to the average salary for architects working in firms with six to eight years' experience, $34,300. This architect must dress exceedingly well because she lives in a world of first impressions. She must entertain because this is where she'll meet and cultivate new clients. If she's smart, she'll send her children to expensive schools where she'll meet wealthy parents, who, thanks to the miracle of childbirth, will be looking for a new room. Yet the architect is still making less than a letter carrier.

All well and good except for one small problem. Responsibility. If the letter carrier misdelivers your mail, someone else receives it. If the architect misspecifies your twenty windows and they come in too small, who pays the $10,000 bill? Architects' insurance is very expensive, and only 24 percent of architects in private practice carry it.

This brings us full circle to our dear owner.

By their nature, people with a surplus of money are savers, often because they were terrorized at some point about not having enough money. Imagine how they'll feel when they begin to contemplate giving as much as $1,000 a day to a dusty, smiling contractor.

Add to this scenario the very real possibility that someone within their immediate family (wife, husband, father, mother) believes that the owners are about to squander their savings. The psychological stress can become too much and often they'll do one of two things:

- Try to do things cheaply. Since they already feel guilty about the decision to redo the bathroom, they decide to punish themselves by doing it in the cheapest possible way. "I did it but I did it for the least possible amount of money, so it's still okay." They try to reuse the rotting vanity, they want to patch the buckling tile rather than replace it. They want to scrape and paint the bathroom themselves. They want to design the project themselves.

  What these owners inevitably end up with is a piece of worthless garbage that they overpaid for. It's still shoddy but now it has no design sense either.

- Or they refuse to deal with the money issue at all. They put themselves deep in denial. They refuse to decide on a budgeted amount that they can comfortably spend. Instead, they want to spend the least amount possible to get the work done, whatever it costs and no more. This is the surest way I know to spend more money on your project than you should.

Owners, architects, and contractors often have dangerous fantasies about the other parties involved. These dreams say, "Find the perfect owner/architect/contractor and all of your money problems will go away without you ever having to face them." For instance:

Contractors dream of mythical wealthy owners who have such great regard for the building trades that money has no value beyond its ability to buy more construction. These great owners fall softly under the contractor's spell, and live to pay for his creation.

The contractor also dreams of the perfect (loyal) architect. During the bidding stage, this architect will tell the client flatly, "This contractor is the finest I've ever met and if you don't hire him I'll resign." At each extra the architect is expected to say, "You're lucky the contractor was able to be so flexible and do this. Pay him what he's asking immediately."

Owners dream that the perfect contractor is out there and that he's the one true craftsman. He's mature, has apprenticed eight years in Maine; he charges fair prices and regards carpentry as his calling. As the job evolves he insists on upgrading things without charge—perhaps only charging occasionally for materials because he understands how much the owners are paying and now asks no more of them. He is only happy to have a job and a chance to practice his religion.

The owners' second fantasy is that when they call in the architect, the architect will have one look around the current home and say, "My God, I have never seen greater natural taste. What gives you the idea that you need professional assistance?" She then walks out, never to be seen again. Or she agrees to help out on the project, do the drawings and other menial work for cost, just so she can have the opportunity to work with the gifted owners.

This dream architect will also know contractors who are so loyal to the architect that they will be willing to perform the work in a matter of days for little more than a few compliments the architect may throw them.

The architect dreams that somewhere there is the client who will make her a star; who is willing to invest the money to fulfill the architect's vision. Architects don't get famous by fulfilling clients' mundane needs and taste. They get famous by developing a vision and then imposing it on every client they can convince to pay for it. Look at Frank Lloyd Wright's beautiful design work. It is simply inspired, a recognizable set of elements worked in endless variation. At a recent show of his work, one of the displays decried the moral turpitude of many of his clients. They had the audacity to alter Wright's interiors by moving furniture or, worse, selling pieces. Some of these clients even tore down walls and raised ceilings. I got to thinking about this while staring at one of Wright's dining room chairs. We've all seen them: tall straight-backs that delineate the dining area with crisp lines. However, as any good furniture maker knows, chair backs have to recline a minimum of 15 degrees to accommodate shoulder blades. Wright's chairs don't, and as a result, they're not comfortable for more than fifteen minutes, but they are beautiful.

Architects dream of finding the owner who will say, "My God, you're a genius. Three bedrooms, a kitchen, family room, dining room, and three and a half baths. Here's the checkbook, see you in six months."

The architect also dreams of the contractor who will absorb the cost of her mistakes. Architects and clients love to believe in the infallibility of architects; that they are all-knowing geniuses who don't make mistakes. *This is not true.* If they are good, they are designing one-of-a-kind solutions to a particular set of problems, and this custom process will, by its nature, generate mistakes. Yet almost all architects are incredibly embarrassed by this. Since the client believes they are geniuses, they like to sweep their mistakes under the rug and they usually view the contractor as that rug. Forgot to include air conditioners on the drawing? The contractor should have known. (Honest to God, an architect once pulled that one on me.) They didn't engineer the specialty window frames completely and it took six days of the contractor's time to remanufacture them at a cost of $3,000? He should realize how important the job is and cover it out of his profit.

These dreams of perfect owners, architects, and contractors are irrational, and they will leave us all feeling continually shortchanged.

3

Solutions to Money Problems

For the owner, one simple action will straighten out 90 percent of the money problems on a job. Set a budget. Set a budget and let everyone know what that budget is. Set a budget and let everyone know that you are not going to exceed that budget under any circumstances. Set a budget and negotiate what you are going to get for that budget. Within that budget are the emergency reserve funds set aside for the inevitable surprises.

Plan your project from beginning to end. Work it all out on paper: and include not only the walls but the rug, the light fixtures, the TV, everything until you have packed the particulars of your dream into your budget. This might seem overly meticulous, but if you want the best deal for your money, this is the way to get it.

But surprisingly, most people are very resistant to doing this because they don't want to see just how much the project is going to cost.

I once worked with a lovely couple who bought an apartment and wanted crown molding from me. We went through my moldings and they settled on a magnificent real plaster molding. It was an incredibly detailed grape leaf design that would wind its way through their entire apartment and cost nearly $12,000. "It's so much money," they said. I lowered my price $1,000 and we went ahead. Once I had finished with the molding, they asked me about the bathroom. They wanted to use honed marble in two subtly different shades, but it would cost $22,000, so I came down $1,500 there. As we finished each element, another part of the apartment would look shoddy in comparison, so we dutifully upgraded it. By the end, they had a magnificent apartment, but it took three times longer than it should have and cost much more than they had ever thought of spending.

Why am I complaining? Because it was wasteful. If they'd been realistic from the beginning about what they wanted, we could have decided on a budget and done the whole renovation in one time period. Instead, I would finish one project, pack up my tools, get called back, do something else, pack up my tools, tear apart a finished wall, put in a new electrical outlet, pack up again, and so on. The entire project took two months longer than it would have and the clients ended up paying twice as much for it than if I had had a proper plan. At the same time, I made less money than if I'd done it all at once; all because the process was inefficient.

Another client had me do a major renovation: Banks of French doors. Inlaid floors. European cabinets. I went back two months later to touch up a chipped door and found no furniture besides folding chairs. They spent every cent they had on construction.

Budgets Define Work

It doesn't matter if the budget is big or small, the important thing is to decide what you can comfortably spend, then plan to spend that amount.

You must tailor your budget to your neighborhood and its property values. Spending $20,000 on a marble bathroom in an area where houses sell for $90,000 makes little sense unless you plan to live there for the rest of your life.

Burdening yourself with uncomfortable debt will also create pain and difficulties that will work their way into the project. You will begin to resent the whole process of rebuilding, and you will scrimp when you shouldn't. You will get angry with contractors and architects but be too embarrassed to tell them why.

You can't tell your contractor who just found two rotting joists that you are going to have to tap your Visa line of credit to have them repaired. Instead, you'll tell him he's an idiot for not noticing them before.

Once you've decided on an amount, it's essential to have professionals help you get the maximum out of that budget. The Hamptons had no way of knowing that buying closeout cabinets wasn't wise. Professionals would have known. Professionals will also know about everything that needs to go into your construction budget. Owners aren't going to know how much a building permit will cost or that installing two new locks could cost $800 or that hanging the $500 drapes could cost another $200.

When I meet people interested in doing work, I ask them what their budget is. Half of them look aghast at me for even asking. They think that if they name the budget, my price will magically come back at that number, plus 15 percent. These people want to believe that by not naming the budget, I might quote a price much lower than the other contractors and still do a very good job. Well, it doesn't work that way. Ironically, without a budget number, we contractors assume *we've* finally found the dream client and add 60 percent to our usual prices.

Owners must tell the architects and contractors their budget number but *make it very clear what it includes*. Tell the architect clearly, "I want to spend ten thousand to fix up my kitchen and dining room. I want it to cover the whole project—design, permits, painting, wall covering, appliances, and an emergency reserve fund of fifteen percent. With the reserve fund, you now only have eighty-five hundred to do the work." If you do this, everyone you're talking to will try to figure out how to fix up your kitchen and dining room for $8,500—and give you the most for your money. Can the budget afford new appliances? Yes. Walls taken down? Probably not. New kitchen floor? Yes. New cabinets? Maybe refacing the old ones instead. All these options can be quickly assessed in reference to how they fit into the budget.

If you don't tell them about the $8,500 or the particulars of what you want and merely ask for a plan to fix up your kitchen and dining room, the architects and contractors are going to go into high gear and tell you how horrible your appliances are, how great granite countertops are, and how many cockroach nests are likely in your kitchen cabinets right now. They want to do a big, beautiful job. Then they'll tell you that they have special places to buy everything where they'll get rock-bottom prices.

They will build such an expensive and perfect dream in your head, all the while telling you, "These marble guys are such a bargain, just wait and see," that when they finally give you a price of $50,000 for all these bargain-basement elements two months from now, you will be thrown in a complete quandary. What is bargain to you and bargain to them could be completely different. Now you either tell them about the $8,500 and have them feel that they've wasted their time or you saddle yourself with such debt that you will never enjoy your dream kitchen and dining room.

But realistically, you may say, "I don't know what an addition costs. I just want to pay the lowest possible price."

With that command, "Get me the lowest possible price," I can build you a plain, ten-by-ten addition that doesn't fit the architecture of your house but will give you another bedroom for $8,000.

Or, with the same command, I could build a twenty-by-twenty addition that improves the silhouette of your house, with custom-milled details to match your existing details, with nice decorative elements on the inside, and a bathroom, and for all of it I'll only charge you 15 percent over cost instead of my normal 22 percent. A true bargain at $44,000.

You know what you can spend. Just start naming figures in large increments—$10,000, $20,000, $4,000?—and you'll quickly find out what price range you're comfortable with.

Now the concern is how you are going to get competitive bids if all the contractors know what the eventual price is going to be. That is simple. People are competing over how much they can *deliver* for a set price, so you'll see the difference between contractors. Setting the price frames the negotiation. Now you can work to get the most out of your money, and each contractor will be forced to creatively solve your needs in a cost-efficient manner.

This is why it's important to find qualified, experienced architects, designers, and contractors. They'll find better ways to solve your problems for less money. They won't have to lower their hourly rate to meet your budget, and they'll find more efficient ways to fulfill your desires, or maybe even a better way to fill your needs.

Recently, I was asked to make a bid to install a bathroom exhaust fan through the facade of a landmarked building. It was going to cost about $6,000 by the time we had an architect, approved plan, sidewalk bridging, and scaffolding.

I asked the clients why they wanted the fan and they told me the paint was peeling in their bathroom from long showers. I suggested they paint the ceiling with epoxy paint. It cost them $250 and now the paint doesn't peel.

Emergency Reserve Fund

Let's talk for a minute about the 15 percent we've set aside as an emergency fund. The challenge for everyone doing a renovation is to have as few unwelcome surprises as possible. In order to do that, the owner, architect, and contractor need to identify as many high-risk areas as possible and explore them in the budget stage so that the 15 percent will be left for the truly unexpected. Therefore, while we're designing our dream kitchen or bathroom, or house for that matter, we need to keep in mind those things that we don't know: What exactly is in the middle of the wall we're planning to move; are there structural elements, pipes, electrical risers? What's underneath the vinyl tile floor in the kitchen? Is that bump in the wall hollow?

If you ask architects about what's in the wall, most will probably shrug their shoulders. They don't want their design to be derailed by a pipe in the wall. Better the owners commit, construction starts, and then deal with it. Ask contractors what's in the wall and most will shrug their shoulders, too. They want to keep their price down now so they get the job. Extras will earn them their profit back later.

Waiting until demolition to discover what's in the wall decreases your leverage. You'll be committed to construction, to this contract, more or less to your contractor's extra prices if you decide to ignore these questions. It could also destroy your 15 percent cushion before you have even started.

Instead, I suggest we find out what's in that wall during the bidding process. Then we can decide whether it makes economic or aesthetic sense to remove it. We should cut some inspection holes and take a look. Perhaps there's nothing. Perhaps there are load-bearing columns for the second floor.

Once we know what's in the wall, we can discuss various design options without the pressure of a crew standing around with hammers in hand.

As well-meaning and helpful as our contractors might be, they are not going to pop that hole in the wall for free—and if they are, they probably won't do a very thorough job of it. Our architect will also probably shy away from beating a hole in the plaster.

I therefore propose the following:

The Rusk Bidding System
----

1. Make a search for a contractor based on a former client's previous experiences with him: his price, his performance, quality, on-time delivery, etc.; and your own comfort with him. (There's a reference checklist in "Solutions to Quality Problems," chapter 11 of this section.)

2. Hire this contractor to work with you during the bidding stage to do the following:

- Assess your preliminary plans to see how well they fit into the proposed budget.

- Knock holes in the walls and investigate existing conditions and how they affect the proposed construction.

- Explore the cost ramifications of various options.

- Once final plans are executed, direct the contractor to make a detailed bid on those plans, including bringing in the necessary subcontractors (e.g., plumbing and electrical).

- Draw up a schedule for the job which the contractor can meet.

All this work can probably be had for $250, and furthermore, you could probably negotiate to deduct $125 from his final price if you go with him in the end. This is a lot of work for $250, but contractors will probably be delighted to do this valuable work because (a) it will make their bid better, (b) they will probably have to do it later anyway, and (c) they are usually asked to do it for free. Even though contractors offer to do this for free, you should pay for it because you'll get a better job, and a contractor who's been paid for his time will feel fairer when it comes time to making prices.

3. Once you have this contractor's bid with itemized prices, bring in at least two other qualified contractors to bid the project, using the specifications of the first contractor to make sure that the other contractors are bidding the same job.

4. Select the best contractor for the job.

The final solution to money problems in the design stage is to separate the project from the money. No amount of money fully pays for what any of us does for a living.

Architects and contractors usually do what they do out of an aesthetic sense, vanity, and a desire to help people. Give them the reins to do that. Help them design a project that will look good in their portfolio. Ask for their knowledgeable help in solving your enormous dilemma of how to get what you want for the price you can afford. When the budget comes in too high, *don't* cut out from the job the one interesting thing the architect has designed. You want to get something interesting—and so does everyone else who works on the project. It will keep their hearts in it once they realize there's no money in it.

4

Time Problems

M any Americans rely on crisis to get things done. They do the things that demand to be done and leave every-thing else to later. Unfortunately, matters of impor-tance are often long-range and don't immediately announce them-selves; but when they do, there's no longer enough time to do them well.

In the design phase, it's likely that the whole process will be put on hold indefinitely. How important is thinking about how we plan to use our kitchen when our child's college application is due in two days? We put it off and put it off and then, when it's time to go away for the summer, we suddenly hunker down to iron out the whole kitchen thing.

Important decisions are slow to make because they require us to first generate many options and then follow them out to their various outcomes. You don't need to make minor decisions this way, but for decisions relating to how you're going to spend your life's savings, it's important that you think through all your options.

When decisions are left to the last minute, people are forced to use the first option that comes to mind and then make an intuitive leap. The result is often the most obvious decision, but rarely is it the best. Time is required to make up a list of options and then research them.

The Hamptons, for instance, have been fighting over how much to spend on cabinets, whether to renovate their kitchen, and whether they should hire a designer. The first step of effective negotiation as taught by the Program on Negotiation at Harvard is to generate as many options as possible without comment. Next, evaluate them. Then, finally, arguments are made to decide which option to use. This process takes time. (And curiously, putting off a decision feels like saving money—a powerful incentive for Mr. Hampton.)

To force some action, Mrs. Hampton demanded that they go to a cabinet store on Saturday and decide. Finally, a crisis that everyone could pay attention to. They arrived, saw a very limited set of options, and from that found a nice set of cabinets about to be sold to someone else. Crisis compounded.

Crisis has made the decision for them. They could either buy the cabinets or fail in their day's unrealistic goal. Rather than facing that, and wanting to feel like winners, they bought the cabinets. Appliance stores and cabinet showrooms know this and they capitalize on it. They set up artificial crises—one-day sales and midnight sales—and then offer their in-house design consultants to allay any last vestiges of common sense left in the poor marks.

The architect's time problems are often intensified because she is often called when owners reach the next crisis level. Usually, it's when the owners have spent most of their allotted design time and they are desperate for professional guidance. Now the architect has to generate a design quickly, relying on hasty impressions of what the owners need and on old solutions to other clients' problems. The custom-fit process that architects and designers offer can still deliver the custom renovation—it just doesn't fit the style of your house.

At the same time, the architect may have another four prospective clients call with the same crisis. Because most architects need the money (and a rushed design takes less time, and therefore will make the architect more money), they will usually take the work and even promise each prospective client their undivided attention.

What usually destroys the schedule during the design phase, though, is the city government's building department. Most owners think they can make design changes up until the hammers start swinging and even then continue to make changes. However, on jobs that require construction permits (and most do) the plans have to be formalized well in advance so that they can be inspected and approved. In New York City, this process takes about a month.

It will feel very wrong for the owners to think that they have to settle on their plan a month ahead of time. It will feel like stopping short of possible perfection. So the owners will usually ask the architect to make a late design change—move the sink, for example—and the architect, whose job is to find the best design and satisfy the client, will probably make the change.

This gives the architect a good excuse to put off filing the building department drawings (which take a lot of time to prepare) and work on this particular design issue. The delay pushes back the issuing of permits and the legal start of construction.

Architects, owners, and contractors allow this to happen because of a very human characteristic. They believe that by crossing their fingers, praying, and applying their own personal luck they'll be able to influence what is beyond their control. They hope that this time the plans will only take one week to get through the building department. Not likely.

Through the design period, the contractor might seem like a character from a Marx Brothers movie. Typically, he's running from job to job, trying to appear calm while aching to duck out so he can yell at someone on his cellular phone. He's probably three quotes behind and coming up with numbers out of the blue sky; making peace at each late appointment by staying longer with the client, only to be even later for the next meeting.

While the contractor does these preconstruction meetings for free, he'll actually get less than half the jobs. As a result, he can spend very little time on each one. The contractor's paying jobs require his undivided attention because on a construction project things are almost always going wrong. This is why one of the Hamptons' contractors missed the first appointment and came two hours late for the next. Most likely, he needed to devote his full time to finishing a previous job, but he made the appointment anyway because his crew was going to be out of work soon and he needed his next project. We call this the Contractor's Dilemma.

Contractors live by both performance and impression. If the contractor has three jobs running concurrently (which is very likely), he needs to give each client the impression that he is overseeing the construction and making sure the architect's intentions are being followed. In reality, he has very little time for that. More likely, he's jumping from job to job, giving the owner a call to ask some small question so that it *seems* he's involved in the minutiae of the project.

As you can see, contractors have little time to spend giving free estimates to people who are "thinking" about renovating their kitchen.

If the client, the architect, and the contractor don't have enough time to do a proper job on the plan the first time, it may well be rejected. Imagine trying to find the time to do it a second time, only better. The contractor is three days late with his other job, and those owners have had to move into a motel. Try to get that contractor to give some prices on your second set of plans.

"Yeah, yeah, yeah. Right, right, right," says the contractor. "Call me in a couple of days."

If the architect worked her heart out on the first plans and the owners reject them, it's not going to be easy for her to sit down again when the best she had to offer was rejected.

At the same time, that great original plan may not have suited the owners—too expensive, wrong style, doesn't match their needs. But because there wasn't time for the architect to do a thorough "needs assessment," she's going to race forward with what makes sense to her. Then, when the client rejects it, the architect can say, "They just don't know what they want."

Time clicks onward.

5

Solutions to Time Problems

Here are the twelve steps of your design phase in chrono-logical order. Understand them and you'll be able to plan your time more effectively.

1. Identify your needs for the renovation.

2. Identify your tastes, making up a clip book from various ar-chitectural photograph magazines.

3. Identify your budget. If necessary, consult your accountant.

4. Identify potential architects and designers by asking friends.

5. Choose an architect based on her reputation, portfolio, price, taste compared to yours, and how you like her personally. This should be an enjoyable process.

6. Begin planning, keeping in mind your needs, your budget, and what you like.

7. Identify contractors, paying particular attention to the recommendations of your architect.

8. Choose a contractor to act as a consultant during the design phase to explore questions about the existing conditions as well as the costs of various options.

9. Explore the different options now rather than later by using mock-ups made by the contractor where possible. These mock-ups will give a better idea of wall locations, table size, counter height, etc.

10. Start the permit and approval process.

11. Decide on a final plan.

12. Have the contractor bid it carefully, calling in his subcontractors and breaking down the bid.

As we discussed in the previous chapter, crisis is often the reason that decisions are made. Therefore, it's necessary to set up a schedule of milestones with actual dates for deadlines. This creates an artificial crisis which we're able to control. Architects love to tell contractors, "I want you to take a look at a job that's going to start on June 1." That firm milestone immediately interests all good contractors.

Deadlines will be invaluable to the health of any construction project. With no deadlines, we naturally hold out for a better solution to our current problem, whether it be which side of the house to put the addition on or what color to paint it. With a deadline, we are forced to choose; deadlines balance our search for the best solution with the time we have to solve it. We have to be willing to sacrifice ultimate perfection in the details for the best possible outcome for the project as a whole.

Here's an example: If I need to add a baby's room addition to my house, I could work and work to come up with the perfect design, a design that suits the house, that maximizes space, that is the most cost-efficient, that can be easily converted into a teenager's room, that will add the maximum value to the house. If I try to achieve 100 percent of my goals for this room, my design won't be done until the baby's toddled off to her first prom. Instead, we must do the best that we can within the time allotted. In this case, we probably don't know about the baby until the third month, don't accept that we need another room until the fourth, and certainly want that room done by the end of the eighth month. That leaves us four months for design, contracting, and construction. We have, then, about two weeks after we've hired the designer to settle on a plan.

As we've noted, contractors and architects are extremely busy people: They have late-breaking emergencies that loom a lot larger than your preliminary design meeting. However, with your desire to satisfy as many goals in the allotted time as possible, you must get your construction team to keep their scheduled meetings. The simplest way is with confirming telephone calls. Now, of course, if you are living in the *This Old House* world, everyone always shows up early, cup of coffee in hand. But you're living in the real world, and even the best contractors and architects are going to occasionally want to miss/avoid/forget/be late for meetings. Your goal is to get the most beautiful project on time and on budget, so accept other people's fallibility and make a few phone calls. They'll do wonders.

The night before a scheduled meeting, give the architect and contractor a call confirming the appointment for the next day. I like to leave a message on their machine or with their secretary so they can't weasel out with some valid excuse. This should be the whole text of the message: "This is Jane Goodman. I'm just confirming we're meeting tomorrow at nine-thirty at my house at 227 Locust Road. I have an appointment at eleven, so I'd appreciate it if you could be prompt. See you tomorrow."

It is very important that you assume they're making the appointment. Don't say, "Just wanted to make sure you'd be there," because it sounds like you expect they might not. Treat your contractor and architect as professionals who never miss a meeting. If they try to excuse themselves out of a meeting, do your best not to let them. They made the appointment, now make them keep it, because it could take another week before you both can meet again. This wasted time will hurt you later, because you'll be forced to make your decisions at deadline before fully examining all the options.

Repeat the address and time for them; slips of paper get lost and address books are left at home. In a perfect world, you shouldn't need to do this, but that shouldn't matter to you. What matters is that you get a beautiful job on time and on budget, and having everyone on time to your meeting is a good start.

If you're really doubtful about someone making an appointment, placing a "question call" the morning of the appointment does wonders. "Hey, Jerry, I know we're meeting at nine-thirty this morning, but I forgot to ask if you could bring a little piece of that green marble with you." This call works a little better if you can talk in person, like at Jerry's house before he leaves that morning.

When you make appointments, listen to what the contractor and architect say regarding their availability. They will likely want to accommodate you and may agree to a time that is inconvenient, and therefore fraught with the possibility that they might miss it. It's best to find a convenient time for everyone. Meetings that occur during a stressful part of the day are rarely relaxed enough to get much work done. One contractor I regularly work with has agreed to several 9:30 meetings with me. He was usually a half hour late to these meetings because he was trying to get all his crew out to jobs. The irony was that while he thought he was being heroic leaving his business unfinished to meet with us, we hated him for being a half hour late.

We now meet in the early afternoon, a time when he's calm, rested, and punctual.

If you want to meet with someone, *never, never* say, "Okay, let's get together sometime next week." It won't happen. It's just another way for people to say, "I don't have time for this." Either meet or don't, but leave nothing up in the air. Otherwise it will certainly cause hard feelings. You may need to say, "I'm not sure how things will go next week, let's say nine-thirty Wednesday and we'll confirm on Tuesday," but even this can cause problems.

It's best to arrange a mutually convenient time to meet and then make that date sacred—like a child arriving at the airport. People need to treat the appointment as a fact and fit their schedule around it.

6

Power
Problems

P ower problems begin when people misjudge the strengths of others and themselves.

In the design phase, owners who are couples will have internal power struggles that will often be the most powerful of their marriage. They are deciding how to spend their savings on their greatest investment. They are defining how they intend to live—at what class/taste/social level. Construction frequently occurs before the birth of a child, and so issues about having children and one's own childhood also enter in. If both partners aren't in sync about these issues, they are going to have to negotiate, and often those negotiations will revert to a pure power struggle. Who makes the money? Who has the inheritance? Who's going to spend most of their time in the house? Who takes care of the kids? Who grew up a certain way? Who doesn't make enough money?

We're also taking the owner's home and transforming it into a dirty, dusty, ripped-apart battleground. During this phase, clients are often forced to live in substandard conditions—they eat a lot of take-out food, use make-do toilet facilities, and have to keep their clothing in boxes and bags. The owners can move in with in-laws (who are, incidentally, very concerned with the amount of money their children are spending to renovate their home).

There are also struggles between the owners and the architect. Let's look at a typical situation. Our husband works hard, advances in his career, and earns a fair salary. His wife, perhaps, also has a fine career, or perhaps has given up that career to raise children, or maybe she's combining both. She brings home an architect or designer, and most likely an alliance is formed. While she advocates for the ideas of the design professional, he might feel left out. Resentment will set in. An architect's perfectly good ideas can become a battleground where people who've felt shut out of the design process can make their fight.

During the design phase, the architect has the power of taste and experience, the owner the power of money and recommendation, the contractor the power of price and objective advice (later on, he'll cease being objective).

7

Solutions to
Power Problems

The solution to power problems lies in the acknowledgment of everyone's strength. Once you locate and respect everyone's part in the relationship, you can turn it to good use for the project.

The powers of architect, contractor, and owner are complementary. Here are the basic roles of the parties.

Owner

- Pays for the work

- Communicates needs, taste, budget

- Chooses personnel for the job

Architect or Designer

- Designs the work

- Finds the needs, taste, and budget of the owner

- Helps owner choose personnel for the job

- Oversees the execution of the work

Contractor

- Executes the work

- Examines the plan for its suitability to serving the needs and budget of the owner as well as assessing its durability

- Makes recommendations for improving and clarifying the plans

If these roles are played fully and with confidence, the project can reach its potential. Confidence is essential. People who feel confident are willing and ready to negotiate with the other players. But those who lack confidence (whether owner, architect, or contractor) will negotiate poorly. They'll be reactive, unwilling to listen to reason, afraid of being taken advantage of.

Confidence is vitally important, so we must constantly work to inspire it in others for our own good. This process of making others feel at ease starts with our first meetings. Reassuring everyone that each has an irreplaceable role in the relationship will make it possible to get the best out of each.

As an owner, you must request the help from the architect that she has to give: "I like so much what you did with the Johnsons' porch that I'm really hoping you can come up with something for the nightmare on the front of our house." The same is true for the contractors. "The Johnsons told me you finished ahead of schedule, with just a few extras, and that you came up with alternatives that really saved them money. I'm all ears for whatever you can suggest." Contractors and architects have to locate and reward the power and skills of the owners as well. Often, their houses aren't decorated well, but their style and taste must be found as well as their primary role acknowledged. For architects and contractors the job here is not to compliment—it's to discover what to compliment; to actively search for what there is to like about an owner's house—and to make mention of it. It's also a good way to learn the owner's tastes.

Once everyone's confident, it's important to discuss everyone's justifiable needs and begin to think about how to fulfill them. By discussing them, we avoid the secrecy that often leads to power struggles. When everyone is up front with what they want and agrees that it is a reasonable and acceptable goal, the secret power struggles usually disappear.

At the design stage the architect wants to design something special. She wants to be paid well for her work, and she wants her finished plans accepted.

The contractor wants the plan to be resolved with all of the details of cabinetwork, materials, and dimensions settled. He wants the design to be sturdy so there'll be no warrantee problems, and he wants to make sure that the owners like the plan.

The owners want a beautiful plan that will suit their requirements for utility for the least possible amount of money and inconvenience.

As none of these desires is mutually exclusive, everyone can work through the design while satisfying their separate goals.

It's also important to establish connections between the players. Hiring a contractor out of the phone book gives you much less power than if you go to the local lumberyard and ask for a recommendation. The contractor out of the phone book can take advantage of you. The contractor the lumberyard recommended had better not take advantage of you because if he does, you'll call the lumberyard and that contractor's source of recommendations will end.

Contractors gain power, too, when an old client recommends a new client. A new client will likely behave well in light of the contractor's relationship with their mutual acquaintance.

These ties encourage people to negotiate through their problems rather than to apply power techniques to make the other side submit. Establish your project as something for the resume. Get pictures taken of the job beforehand and document the process so that later the professionals can use the work in their portfolios.

8

Management
Problems

M anagement is really the art and science of establishing structures that handle little problems before they cause big problems. Robert Pirsig in *Zen and the Art of Motorcycle Maintenance* called these small problems Gumption Traps. In his classic example, Pirsig was trying to remove a nut from his motorcycle engine. He didn't have the right-size wrench, so he searched around and found something close. The wrench slipped and rounded off the nut. Once he'd done that, even if he found the correct-size wrench, it wouldn't fit. Then, once he managed to hammer it off with a pair of vise grips, he'd have to go to the motorcycle shop and order a new nut. Contemplating his rounded-off nut, he'd find a reason to go to the bathroom or to make a phone call and probably wouldn't face his motorcycle for the next several weeks.

Likewise in renovation, there is a great impetus toward inertia. Phone numbers are lost, written-down specifications are buried in one of three file folders, and the only decent hardware store that shows decorative doorknobs may be ten miles away and they're out of everything but brass plate.

Typically, the owners are often embarrassed by their own ignorance. They've never done a renovation before, they don't know what their role is, and other than what well-meaning friends have passed on, they have no idea how to hire an architect or designer, or even tell the difference between them. They don't know how long things should take or what they should cost. They have no means of evaluating bids. Because they don't understand these things, owners themselves are a source of inertia.

Owners sometimes view the architect as the expert who'll handle what things should look like, what they should cost, and how long it should take.

Unfortunately, architects, like contractors, have a vested self-interest in the project. There's a great Romanian restaurant in New York where all you need to do is walk in the door and say feed me—no ordering—and they'll take care of everything. It's a lot of fun—they bring the bottle of vodka embedded in a block of ice, they'll bring appetizers, main course, dessert, aperitif. Indulgence without responsibility.

But there are a few problems. It will take the rest of the night, so if you had other plans, you're in trouble. The food is good, but probably not exactly what you were thinking of; and the bill is very high. That bottle of vodka was $80 alone. But that's not to say that this restaurant is doing business in bad faith. They are assuming that you like the food, you have the time, and you have the money.

For a night, it's fine to be swept away. Two hundred fifty dollars is a lot of money, but it's manageable. This isn't the way to do a renovation, though. Architects and contractors *need* your direction to give you what you want, when you want it, and for what you want to pay.

An architect's management problems start at the first meeting where her goal must be to get the job. Owners will tend to hire the architects who endorse the owners' plan. So it's quite possible the architect will find herself saying, "Yes, we can do what you want for the money you want to spend." It's only after she's gotten the job that the architect realizes that there's not enough time or money, that the basic idea of the job is faulty. It is then difficult for her to go back and change what she has agreed to, so she must try to get contractors to conform to what she needs.

Contractors are typically inclined to conform to designer's needs. They are, for the most part, helpful people who are out pushing cars out of snowbanks in the winter. This helpfulness can lead them to go along with architect's plans that are out of sync with reality during this design phase. It's often not until the actual contracting stage when they deliver their final budget that they start raising prices to conform to the real world.

The owner tries to be "helpful" as well. Not the good kind of helpful that this book is about, but the bad kind of helpful. The kind that says, "Oh, that's okay, no big rush." Or "No problem, we'll figure it out when we get to it." The problem with this approach is that contractors and architects are constantly performing a kind of triage. Whatever area of their business is causing them the most pain gets the attention for the minute. If the owner takes off the pressure to perform, then the contractor may put his attention to a job elsewhere. While the owner was trying to be "nice," he's going to end up screaming.

And all three of our partners are overworked.

The architect has four jobs with various emergencies which he must coordinate. The contractor has as many emergencies to coordinate, but he has to fix them as well.

Both of them have answering machines full of messages from people who have problems on old work and problems with the work being done right now. They also have people who want them to look at new work.

Meanwhile, the owners, who before the renovation were busy keeping the plates of family, career, and social obligations spinning, must now add in the plates of architect, contractor, budget, taste, and shopping. And we are about to take away the place they usually do their plate spinning, not to mention most of their money.

All of these issues are the underlying cause of poor management. It is the lack of time, money, and willpower that prevents the elements of the job from being organized into a clear plan.

9

Solutions to Management Problems

First, get everyone to read this book.

Next, look for the problems that are impeding the flow of the project. Imagine that your job is to walk from one end of a prison to another. As you walk, a series of gates must be opened, one after another, and in many places there is more than one gate to choose. We will give you a walkie-talkie, and with it you will be able to reach a guide who's familiar with the prison. After listening to her advice, you will make a decision about which gate to open, and you'll tell the guide, who will relay your decision to the gatekeeper, who will open the gate.

If everyone is working together, you will make your way smoothly through the prison. If the guide leaves her walkie-talkie for a while, or gives you some bad advice, or you describe your location incorrectly, or the gatekeeper opens the wrong gate, you might spend the night.

In a construction project this is what will slow you down:

- The owners don't have the information to make the decision.

- The owners don't know they have a decision to make.

- The owners are afraid to commit to a decision for fear they're wrong.

- The owners are afraid to commit to the whole project because they're afraid of the money, the renovation, or the proposed change to their whole life.

- The owners' decision involves unappealing options. *(Q.* Do you want the brown or the black leather on the chrome dining room chairs? *A.* Neither. I don't want a high-tech kitchen, we need to look at antique sets.)

- The architect is too busy to give the information quickly.

- The architect fails to realize that the clients need colored, perspective drawings in order to make their decisions.

- The project is going in a direction the architect feels is unappealing.

- The architect doesn't feel she's being paid enough to generate all the options and give the owners all the information they need.

- The contractor, without getting paid, is resistant to generating prices so that the owners can make their decision.

- The contractor feels the project is too large or too small or out of his realm.

- The contractor is too busy, too deep in debt, doesn't like the clients, or has a better job lined up.

When things start to move slowly, analyze the problem with this list and then address it. Keep yourself fed with information so that you can make the timely decisions that will keep your project moving.

Providing you get the information you need, how do you go about making decisions? The simplest way is to list all the positives and negatives and assign a monetary value to each. Add this to the monetary value of the work and you should find your solution. For instance:

I've got a rotten old shed on my property. Should we tear it down and build a new one, renovate the shed we have, or purchase a cheap tin shed?

Tear down and build new

Property value improvement	+$3000
Utility	+1000
Cost of new shed	-2500
Time to build new shed	-600
Cost of laying out $2,500	-400
NET VALUE	**+$500**

Renovate shed we have

Property value improvement	+$1800
Utility	+600
Cost of work	-1800
Time to renovate	-600
Cost of laying out $1,800	-300
NET VALUE	**-$300**

Tear down shed, put up cheap metal shed

Property value improvement	+$300
Utility	+500

Cost of work	**-600**
Time to build	**-200**
Cost of laying out $600	**-100**
NET VALUE	**-$100**

These determinations are arbitrary, but they show that the new shed is the only thing that has a positive value. Now, by shifting values, or by adding new categories, we may shift the final outcome; but some method must be followed to make construction decisions and this is a good one to work with. It takes into account cost of construction, value of money, resale value, cost of time, and utility. What's surprising here is that throwing up a metal shed did better than renovating the old one. That was because it was very expensive to renovate the old, with little increase in property value and utility. Building a new storage shed improved resale value and utility a great deal, enough to offset my uncomfortableness in spending the money to renovate.

It's now time to talk about the difference between architects and designers. Up until now, I've grouped them together as design professionals or I've just said "architects."

An architect has gone through an architecture program at the college or university level, understands local code and rudimentary engineering, and has passed a very rigorous examination in most locales. They have at their disposal the American Institute of Architects, which provides general support services and reasonably fair contracts for work (though they absolve the architect of most responsibility).

Designers, on the other hand, may not be licensed in your area and may have come to design any number of ways. Their specialty is to make things look attractive, and more than their credentials, you'll want to look at their portfolio to see if their taste suits yours. For the most part, designers will be skilled with color, fabric, window treatments, and furniture. Along with these base skills (skills many architects lack), some also have construction skills. I've known designers who've designed molding, moved walls, designed kitchens, etc. For much of that work, they'll need to use a licensed architect or engineer to sign off on their plans to obtain a permit.

Designers tend to create their environments by color, fabric, and furniture, whereas architects will be more likely to manipulate space. Architects have an intimate and complete knowledge of the construction end of the work as well as a developed aesthetic sense of space and detail. Because they understand how things go together, they can make rational plans that are acceptable to contractors.

Architects are usually more expensive, though there is a set of "star" designers in every town who determine the local style and whose fees are commensurate with the exclusivity of the trends they are setting.

Sometimes, architects are hired to design and build the project, and a designer sympathetic to the architect's work is hired to finish and furnish it.

Start a three-ring notebook now with all of the paperwork and notes that your project will generate. It's better than loose files because it will be more accessible during meetings. By the end of the project, it will be a battered and interesting testament to your project. Along with pictures of stoves, "to-do" lists, and contracts, keep your own list of changes and their costs as you go along, especially for changes for which no formal change order was made. This will save you money at the end of your project. The contractor may forget that the reason he never charged you for moving the toilet was that it saved him from having to run a new vent line.

Likewise, for your own sanity, keep a list of payments and what they were for.

10

Quality
Problems

Quality is expensive. It costs money and time. Quality requires very careful management and impeccable application of power to achieve.

Quality also doesn't reveal itself all at once:

- Quality of finish is immediately notable. Are the seams in the granite tight and even? Is the grout between the tiles regular? Is the paint on the doors smooth?

- Quality of visual design will also be immediately notable. Is the room attractive? Do colors and forms work together? Do things feel lopsided?

- Quality of functional design will reveal itself within six months. Is the refrigerator too far away? Is there room behind the door for towels? Can my daughter use the sink?

- Quality of underlying structure will take a few years to become obvious. Are ceramic tiles secure or do they come loose? Have the doors warped because they weren't adequately primed? Does the sink clog up because the existing drain pieces were reused rather than replaced?

The work that goes into ensuring long-term quality can seem picky. The owner wants to keep the budget reasonable, so why are we wasting time redesigning cabinets for two inches? Why does the plumber want to spend $1,000 ripping up all the perfectly good drains? Why do we have to use a cabinet shop that is twice as expensive for producing cabinets with the same specifications?

Quality also relates to customer service. A reputable contractor will return to replace the tile that loosens because he budgets for it. The lowball contractor may not have the money in his bid to fix things. The architect who agrees to a low price may not be able to afford to do three different plan variations, let alone seven. She may offhandedly recommend that the owners might want to pick up their own hardware and light fixtures to save money. The quality designer won't do that.

"What's wrong with choosing your own hardware and light fixtures?" you're asking. There shouldn't be anything wrong, but there is a difference between the light fixtures that architects working with clients hand me and the fixtures that clients working on their own discover. The cost may be the same, but architects have sources unavailable or unknown to clients and have a better sense of the overall style of the renovation. Clients working alone often find themselves in home improvement stores listening to salespeople who don't have much design sense.

The problem is the cost. Picking out the correct hardware is going to cost a lot of money in relation to the item's cost. Let me explain. If the architect charges $75 an hour, buying $50 of drawer pulls could end up costing $275. You could have purchased them for $50. The problem is, you probably wouldn't have chosen those handles. You'll likely see all the choices available, get confused, and either pick the safest thing possible or the thing you saw in a stylish magazine. If a renovation project is to have a positive effect on the value of your house, it must have an integrated design, one that harmonizes with itself and with the existing structure. It requires as much training and natural talent to do that as it takes to vocally harmonize. Consider your drawer pulls and lighting fixtures as the final voices added to your house. They can bring the music either to a crescendo or to an awkward, inglorious end.

In the big picture, an $80,000 renovation can be made perfect by another $500 worth of expensive, heavy, well-designed hardware.

Quality in execution is very expensive. Let's look at the painting of a door. Method A: Roll on a primer, roll on two coats of paint. Touch up around doorknob and hinge with a brush. Method B: Remove hardware. Sand door. Remove door from hinges and prime bottom and top with an oil-based primer to prevent moisture from getting into door and warping it. Rehang door and oil prime using an underbody paint. Use brush to smooth out paint. Return the next day and sand. Use tack cloth to remove dust. Apply first finish coat with additive. Use brush to smooth out paint. Return next day and sand. Use tack cloth to remove dust. Apply final coat with additive. Use brush to smooth out paint. Reinstall hardware.

Do people regularly specify how this door is to be painted in the contract? No. It is a matter of ethics on the part of the painter.

Quality is a matter of ethics. It is what often separates a good architect from a kitchen designer at a lumberyard. Most lumberyard kitchen designers are there to move product. They have read sales manuals from the manufacturer and they are there to convince you to buy what they have to sell. It may be a great match. It may be a horrible match.

Architects and designers often hobble their own process in an effort to get hired. Prospective clients don't know how to judge architects—all they know is that they want something nice and they don't want to spend a lot of money to design it. Along comes an architect who quickly sizes them up and comes up with some good first suggestions. That kind of quick designing seems to bode well for the rest of the process, our owners think. But this thirty minutes of chatting can define the next four months of work. The "Versailles look" may sound great this evening, but three and a half months from now when the bids come in, Versailles might look too heavy and French. Settling on a design direction the first night may feel wonderful, but in fact you've just short-circuited the design process. You've missed the opportunity to find something that is *exactly* right for you.

Unfortunately, the time it takes for an architect to find what you want can feel very risky to the owners. What if after three meetings, the architect doesn't deliver anything? What if, in fact, she has no ideas?

Likewise the contractor asked to give a ballpark price as the design is formalized is throwing together numbers and ideas because he doesn't have the time or the money to do it well. He needs to get on to the next bid of the day, then on to the job sites he's running right now. The information he's giving, the rough estimate of $10,000 to do labor for the kitchen, could be off by 50 percent but it doesn't really matter to him. He's not being paid to give a ballpark price, and he couldn't really bring in his plumber and electrician every time he wanted to make a bid. What if the job never happens or he gets too busy to even take it? And what about the other two contractors who've been asked to give a ballpark price? If his price is higher than the two other contractors because he's thought these things through, he might be out of the bidding before there's even a real set of plans. It is not in his best interest, as things stand, to give a realistic and probably higher budget.

The problem comes when the owner uses these three ballpark budget numbers to make design and budget decisions. The owners may allocate their budget of $27,000 as follows.

Basic contracting
(demo, walls, plumbing,
electricity, floors,
and paint)   **$10,000**

Viking stove	**3,000**
Other appliances	**1,000**
Rutt cabinets	**9,000**
TOTAL	**$23,000**
Reserve	**4,000**
GRAND TOTAL	**$27,000**

Since the contracting wasn't that expensive, they've gone with the very expensive stove and cabinets. They'll now spend time deciding on finishes for the cabinets, picking stainless-steel splashes to go with the stove, and haggling over a wallpaper that will harmonize with the pickled finish on the cabinets. They'll pay the architect to draft the bid documents and construction drawings and send them out.

Imagine their unhappiness when the least expensive contractor's price comes in at $15,000, blowing their budget apart. Now what? They'll scramble to find cheaper alternatives to the Rutt and the Viking, and then recoordinate their wallpaper and everything else. They'll probably start late and without all the decisions made, which will result in more extras as things must be changed during the job to make it all work together again.

You may also have a good contractor, but one who is wrong for the job. If you're planning on a showplace $20,000 bathroom and your brother-in-law recommends his great contractor, you may be inclined to go along with him—especially when he turns in a nice professional bid and his other references are just as enthusiastic. It will surprise you, then, when you come home and find he's installed the marble tiles in a haphazard fashion, paying no attention to their veining or color variations. Additionally, he's made a mess in your bedroom outside the bathroom, and he's been complaining about how little money he's making.

On investigation, you may discover that all the fine work he's done has been for restaurants. Sure, he's done marble work, but not with any real artistic intention. He hasn't done residential work and, in fact, has no concept of working in an occupied apartment. His jobs have an average budget of $120,000, and he's been able to manage them from his office. Your tricky little $20,000 job has required him to come on-site almost every day.

The last quality problem is caused by good design that has custom-built, one-of-a-kind elements. The more unusual these bits are, the more likely that they won't come out right and will have to be adjusted during construction, resulting in extras for you.

11

Solutions to Quality Problems

To achieve quality, we have to choose the right people to work with; people with a natural impetus toward doing their best. We can either trust our intuition, take a look at their briefcase and shoes, and go with that, or we can use a far more safe, powerful, and realistic tool.

We need to have the courage to call references and ask them questions.

Designer Reference Checklist

1. What was the size and type of the job and the level of perfection required?

2. How did she work with you to come up with a design?

3. How satisfied were you with that design?

4. How organized was she in keeping design decisions, needs, money, contractors, and contracts straight?

5. Were there problems or complaints from the contractor with how things were designed to be built?

6. What kind of problems have you had with the project since completion?

7. Did you enjoy working with her?

Once you've asked at least three former clients for responses to these questions, you'll have a good idea of whether or not you want to work with this architect or designer. It's unlikely that an architect is going to receive a perfect score on this test. If she does, you're probably not getting a totally honest response—the owner being interviewed feels he owes the architect a favor and is trying to sell you. Let the reference know that you can't count any 100 percent positive response. Find out what the architect's weaknesses are, because once you know those weaknesses, you can give the architect you hire the opportunity to improve on your project. "The people I spoke to really have a lot of respect for your design skills. They seemed less sure of your management skills. What are you currently doing to improve that?"

This designer now knows you mean business, that you want all of the design skills she's exhibited in the past but that you also are requiring her to be well organized. By your bringing it up before you start, she is agreeing to work to a higher standard. You're doing her a great favor as well. When the next prospective client calls the designer's last three references and the first two condemn her management skills and then you let the caller know how diligently she worked to control the project, she stands a better chance of getting the job.

Asking the size and type of a designer's former jobs is very important to see how your project lines up with what she's done before. You must be very careful about hiring someone out of her usual area of expertise. Her quality level, prices, and management style will likely be out of sync with your project.

Next, we must call the contractor's references.

Contractor Reference Checklist

----

1. What was the size and type of the job and the level of perfection required?

2. How accurate and complete was his budget and did he price alternate plans?

3. How did he respect time constraints, from appointments to deadlines?

4. How organized was he in keeping design decisions, finishes, plans, and contracts straight?

5. Were there problems or complaints from the architect over how things were built?

6. What kind of problems have you had with the project since completion?

7. Did you enjoy working with him?

Again, it's important to pay attention to the sizes of jobs he is used to working on and how fussy he's been. A great mason contractor used to pouring sidewalks may not be the great mason contractor you need for mosaic tiling your bathroom.

Finally, contractors and designers need to ask the same questions of professionals who have worked with these owners before, and the owners need to ask the same questions of themselves.

Owner Reference Checklist

----

1. How clear were they on their budget and were they willing to communicate that?

2. How did they respect time constraints—making decisions, keeping appointments?

3. How organized were they in keeping design decisions, finishes, plans, and contracts straight?

4. Did they make many changes during the design phase? How about the construction phase?

5. Were they willing to pay for changes?

6. How were they to work with? How did they respond to advice and adversity?

Sometimes, just asking these questions will lead you to improving the quality of your project because they help to set goals and mileposts. In fact, it wouldn't be a bad idea to post these at the job for a while so people can tell what criteria they are being judged by.

Calling references will also give you more leverage. A contractor or architect will likely give you references that are satisfied customers. If that contractor or architect then turns around and does a bad job for you, you are likely to call back their satisfied customer and complain—in effect ruining this reference for future customers. The contractor or architect who knows you contacted their best clients will treat you as if you were referred by them. They will work much harder to maintain a good reference.

Once we've interviewed references, we need to look at portfolios and perhaps visit prior jobs. Portfolios will establish the level of the work, but it's difficult to tell that the doors don't shut well from a photograph. When you visit a previous job, look for anything that's falling apart: tiles coming up or cracking, doors that are out of alignment, counters that have gaps or are misaligned, paint that is coming up.

Also look for things that point to poor craftsmanship: tile floors that show a bumpy surface underneath; plastered walls that aren't smooth; runs and sags in the paint; open joints in the woodwork.

Check the operation of doors and the general feel of the kitchen to work in. Quality of design is difficult to evaluate in a short visit, but try to imagine working in the kitchen; see if it overcomes the defects inherent in its physical peculiarities. Does the galley kitchen feel cramped or pleasantly cozy? Does the L-shaped kitchen feel disjointed or systematized?

If the owners are there, ask them what they would change in the design if they had to do it again.

Checking references is the first hurdle. Next, check with the Better Business Bureau for any problems as well as the city government to see if there are any outstanding liens against the contractor and whether he is licensed. You may even want to do a credit check. It is difficult and time-consuming to hide poor past performance (usually a result of being poorly organized). If he was inept on the job, he's probably inept at hiding it as well.

To get quality, we must establish criteria for quality. There are two types of quality we are concerned with: quality of workmanship and quality of materials. While we're cruising through the portfolio and the job sites, we must begin to set our own standard of quality. Is the slightly rough texture of this paint job acceptable? Can you live with Formica countertops or must they be granite?

In my experience, high-quality materials with poor or even medium workmanship is worthless. I've seen marble bathrooms that were so clumsily done that it would be better to just tear them out and put in ceramic.

My advice is to insist on top-quality workmanship and a minimum of sturdy, well-made materials. Then, if there is still money, work up to more expensive materials. If you can't afford that minimum, don't bother to do the work.

We want doors that align, plaster that's smooth, countertops that are level. We may like granite countertops but our budget may preclude them. Or we may be willing to sacrifice some other part of the job to allow us to put granite in the kitchen.

Luxury materials are more expensive for a few reasons. They are actually more expensive because of their scarcity. (Compare the number of known granite quarries to known Formica quarries worldwide. Frightening.) Moreover, luxury materials are often fabricated to order. If you want a cheap countertop, you can go to the lumberyard and buy a piece of "Postform" counter in standard white, twenty-four inches deep, which they cut from a sixteen-foot blank they keep out back. Then put it in the trunk. If you want granite countertops, you'll need to look through samples of granite, choose a particular slab, have templates made of your cabinets, have it cut, the edges polished, and then have it delivered.

Luxury materials also require more labor to install. Cheap cabinets from the lumberyard will screw onto the walls in a few minutes. Expensive custom cabinets are going to have more trim pieces, which are cut on-site.

Luxury materials aren't necessary for a beautiful renovation. I've seen beautiful bathrooms in white ceramic tile. The first order of beauty is in the workmanship.

Quality in execution will mean nothing if you don't like the design; so first, understand the design. This is no simple task. Few clients can look at a set of blueprints and understand what they are getting. *Insist* on colored, perspective drawings of different views of your project. If the architect doesn't have the skills to make them, either get computer-generated versions or arrange to have the architect commission them.

Finally, to get good quality, speak to your consulting contractor to find what problems he sees in executing the plans. Unusual, one-of-a-kind elements are the hallmark of good design, and I strongly advocate for having some of these elements worked into your renovation. I also advocate that you review it with your contractor so that he can work out the kinks before it is built. Extra costs are likely in most construction jobs, but the more your contractor can plan ahead, or adjust the design so that he can use more standard materials or methods, the fewer extra costs you'll incur.

Now would be a good time to look at the Materials section in the appendix of this book.

12

The Finleys— Planning for a Dream Kitchen

Tom Finley was looking at his walls and realizing they were kind of crooked. The hard part was deciding whether that bothered him or not. In a way, it was kind of homey (the holes in his oldest jeans didn't bother him either). On the other hand, the crooked walls made the cabinets sit crooked.

He and his wife had been trying to decide what to do with the kitchen. They could leave it as it was and save the money; they could put some new doors on the cabinets; they could renovate the whole kitchen; or they could simply move out of the house, leaving it behind like a snake's old skin. But Tom didn't want to do that. Tom wasn't completely sure why this was all so important, but it was. He also wasn't sure why this was taking so much time, but it was.

The Finleys' house was interesting. They lived in a nice neighborhood of older houses, and the exterior of their house was in beautiful, cared-for shape. But the kitchen was a disaster. The previous owner had decided to put in a new kitchen before he sold it, so he ripped out the old tile on the floor and walls, took down the old cabinets with glass doors, and threw out all the old appliances. Then he set about buying the very cheapest things he could find to put in their place. The people who'd installed the kitchen apparently didn't have a level, so the cabinets followed the crooked walls and floor. They also didn't use very good anchors for the cabinets, and one had fallen the year before; Tom had fixed it with some now-yellowed packing tape. The countertops had big gaps behind them where pencils and cheese were regularly swept. The kitchen had no unique style: beige cabinets, beige counters, neutral, "sellable," and ugly. The result turned out to be a damper on the former owner's hopes of selling the house. The kitchen looked cheap and the prospective buyers who walked through the house couldn't bear the sin of tearing out a brand-new kitchen. The Finleys bought the house for the rest of its charms, fixed what needed fixing everywhere else, and put off renovating the new kitchen until it wasn't quite so new.

Now Tom sat back in his chair. He'd take a quick nap and think about the crooked walls.

Michelle Finley couldn't bear thinking about the kitchen. When they had moved into the house, she tried to look happy, but she shuddered nearly every time she walked into the kitchen. They had looked at so many houses with nice kitchens—and it wasn't that she spent so much time there, but this kitchen, with its bumpy floors and masking tape, depressed her.

But the most depressing thing of all was that they'd been living here for five years and they hadn't done anything with the kitchen. Should they just sell the place or put in a new kitchen and stay? She loved her neighbors, and their kids, John and Leslie, had a pack of friends in the neighborhood. She hated the thought of moving.

The problem, though, was renovating the kitchen. She had heard so many nightmares from her neighbors about remodeling jobs that dragged on for months, and about contractors that didn't even stay on the job. She'd also heard horror stories about architects and contractors getting together to rip off owners, by using $200 towel bars and then each of them charging 20 percent on top of that, so one towel bar ended up costing $280. Three hundred with tax.

People spent a lot of money on these renovations and Michelle was worried that the money would just disappear and they wouldn't have anything to show for it. She was afraid they'd end up with something as ugly as what they had now. Tom and Michelle had been to Jack's Lumber to see about doing it themselves—and found Jack a total sleazeball. It seemed to them that he had a lot of closeout kitchens that weren't much better than what they had now—at least their current kitchen cabinets filled in the walls somewhat. Jack's closeout cabinets fit his showroom and that was it.

This left the Finleys somewhat perplexed. Were Jack's customers supposed to put a couple of his kitchens together like Neapolitan ice cream? Dark-stained oak by the refrigerator, white Melamine by the window, and pink Formica around the sink?

The Finleys also had a time deadline to consider. If they were going to redo their kitchen, they wanted to do it during the summer, five months away. From the people they talked to, they knew that five months wasn't that long to decide on an architect, a contractor, and a design, let alone get the permits. So they set today aside to decide what they were going to do.

Across town, Giovanni DeTomaso was sitting in his shop, sharpening a chisel. He liked to sharpen tools. He liked to protect sharp tools and he liked everyone who worked for him to bring their own sharp tools so they didn't borrow his and make them dull. DeTomaso hated to find his chisel rounded off thanks to some amateur beating it against a cement wall.

DeTomaso enjoyed working with clients who appreciated his precision; who didn't try to hammer *him* into a cement wall.

Two years before, DeTomaso had taken two weeks off and thought about his business. He thought about what he was doing wrong and what he was doing right. His son Leonardo (also in the business) wrote down these ideas, and together they decided upon a few strategies for making themselves the most money in the long run. They both knew that a company with the best reputation would have a steady referral of new jobs. During the lean times, when jobs were scarce, they would have to take bad jobs, and bad jobs never make money. Giovanni had been around long enough to know how to spot a bad job: They were with stupidly cheap or meanspirited clients, they had sloppy architects or designers, they didn't have enough money in them for the time needed to complete them, they were poorly designed and ended up looking terrible. DeTomaso hated bad jobs, so he sat down with Leonardo and they came up with some rules to avoid them:

1. Get paid for bids. Then take the time to figure the bid carefully. Treat the bidding process with the same set of criteria as the job: quality, thoroughness, long-range thinking. Bring the plumber and the electrician into the bidding process so you get reliable numbers from them. Call up the suppliers. Force the architect or designer or owner to nail down as many specifications as possible.

2. Never start a job without all decisions made. A job that gets going without key decisions made is a bad risk. If the client can't finish the design stage in time for bidding, then the construction stage won't finish on time either. The job will go over the time budgeted and the contractor will lose the money.

3. No matter how highly DeTomaso and Son were recommended, always insist that the owners get at least one additional bid. Otherwise, the owner might be suspicious. DeTomaso protects himself by having the owner give the other contractor his complete estimate breakdown (without the prices) so that the other contractor can't substitute less thorough methods or cheaper materials. DeTomaso always warns his customers he will be higher than the competition, but this way the owners know by how much.

DeTomaso gave his manifesto to everyone who called for his services. He liked being treated as a professional, and when treated as a professional, he delivered.

DeTomaso started to rub his chisel across a diamond honing board until the edge of the chisel was smooth as glass and he could see his face in the edge. He slid the chisel into an old piece of maple and a long curling strand came off the wood. He turned off the lights and brought it into the house to show his son.

"If we move, how much money are we going to get out of the house? What we paid for it? We haven't really done that much to it," Michelle said.

"But would you want to do the kitchen and then move and let someone else enjoy it?" Tom asked.

"No, that's what I'm saying. We might as well do the kitchen and then stay here."

"But how are we going to do the kitchen? We don't just *do* the kitchen. It's going to cost time and money."

Michelle looked at Tom. "It seems fairly simple. Let's just decide how much time and money we can spend on the kitchen and see what we can get for that."

Tom shook his head. "How can we know what it will cost?"

"That's not the point. We can only spend so much time and so much money on this. Let's decide how much time and money we have, and that will help us decide what kind of kitchen we should get."

"But I don't know how much we have to spend on a kitchen," Tom protested.

"Two thousand? Five thousand, ten thousand, twenty—"

"No, definitely not twenty thousand."

Michelle smiled. "Ten thousand?"

Tom looked at the kitchen. "How much is the house worth right now?"

"Probably what we paid for it, one hundred and twenty thousand."

"And what are the other houses around here selling for?"

"One-seventy-five to two-twenty."

"Really, who sold for two-twenty?"

"The Kramers. They had the three-car garage and the beautiful kitchen. Four bedrooms, too."

"So what do you think we could sell our house for if we had a beautiful kitchen?"

Michelle thought about their house. They'd repainted, done the floors, all the doors worked. The bathrooms were original but nice quality. "Maybe one-sixty or one-seventy."

"So you're saying a new kitchen might boost our house value up forty or fifty thousand dollars?" Tom said.

"I'm not necessarily saying that. We could talk to a real estate person and see what they say. But as long as we don't spend thirty or forty thousand dollars, I don't think we'll be wasting money."

"And how much time?" Tom asked.

"Do you have time to do this yourself?" Michelle asked. "I certainly don't."

"No, forget doing it ourselves," Tom said. "I'm not going to spend the next two years of weekends hating you and this house and trying to learn how to hang wallpaper and install molding. Not me. Remember Hank and Andrea? They did it themselves before they sold their house and the couple who finally bought the house made them rip out the whole kitchen before they would close. That's the problem with this kitchen right now. It's a complete 'do-it-yourself.' "

"Who sucked the old brain out of my husband and gave him sense?"

Tom laughed. "If we're going to do the kitchen, let's just hire professionals and do it right. I'll meet weekends, evenings, talk on the phone, but I think we should have professionals do this. Do we hire an architect or designer—or do we just hire a contractor?"

Michelle started to reach for the phone book, then thought better of it. "I think we should ask some people who've done this before—see who has used designers, architects, who just used contractors. I wouldn't mind saving the money by not using an architect, but I don't know. What are you smiling at?"

"Remember those people over on Ivy?" Tom said.

"Who?"

"With the deck?"

Michelle started to laugh. "The deck with the house, you mean? I have never seen more deck in my life. It looks like an environmental zoo with a nice walkway all around to view the inhabitants."

"I think they skipped the architect and just got the decking contractor."

"Yeah, maybe we want some professional design help. Let's ask around."

"Fine," Tom said.

"By when?"

"Let's each have a list of three contractors and three design professionals by next Saturday."

Michelle made a face. "Do they have to be 'design professionals' or could they just be architects and designers?"

"Shut up."

"Wait, how much do we want to spend?" Michelle asked.

"I don't know. No more than twenty thousand?"

"Why don't I talk to Rosenwasser and see how much he thinks we should spend?"

"Why bother an accountant?"

"Because it's his business."

Tom was watching Michelle, who was looking at her list. "Did everyone say 'DeTomaso' to you?" Michelle asked.

"Two people said he was too expensive."

"Did they have good people?"

Tom laughed. "No, both of them said they couldn't recommend their contractor because he left things half finished, took forever, and did a mediocre job."

Michelle said, "I got a few others, but the people who hired DeTomaso said he was very good. He also apparently has a pamphlet he gives out."

"Really? Well, let's get ahold of him."

"He also charges two hundred and fifty for an estimate."

"Forget that," Tom said. "Nobody charges for an estimate."

"He takes it out of his bid if you hire him."

"That's ridiculous," Tom said. "What do I get for my two-fifty?"

"Apparently he'll knock holes in the walls, floors and ceiling, if the architect has any questions about structure or plumbing. He breaks everything down carefully and he's willing to give alternate pricing schemes."

"What do the architects think of him?"

"I don't know. Did you get any good architects?"

Tom referred to his list. "I got three. Two sound good."

"Me too. So now what?"

"It seems to me, first we interview architects and designers—see who we want. Then ask them for contractors that they've worked with."

"Oh," Michelle said, "that's a good idea. Maybe someone besides DeTomaso at least. Do we invite over all six architects?"

"I don't have the time for that."

"How about we call each of them up, chat on the phone, tell them what our budget is—"

"What's our budget?"

Michelle flipped over her pad. "Rosenwasser said that if our neighborhood is as good as we say it is, we should put the money into the kitchen. Put enough so that it looks really nice and becomes an asset to the house. If we spend too little, we're better off doing nothing and planning on selling the house for what we paid for it."

"So how much, Michelle?"

"He recommended twenty-five to thirty with some fancy things. He said we had enough to spend fifteen from savings and he recommended selling some things we don't need for another five and borrowing the final five."

"What do we have to sell for five thousand dollars?"

"That's what I said. He said look around, you'll find something. I talked to a real estate person, too."

"Michelle," Tom said, nodding his head, "nice."

"Thank you. She said people looking in this neighborhood want to see built-in appliances, nice counters, Corian or granite, they want to see center islands, and they want to see size."

"Damn. We don't have size."

"Den, Tom. The den. No one uses it, it's packed with junk. Garage-sale all that junk and move half the kitchen in there."

"Let me think," Tom said. "So, we call up architects and designers and we tell them twenty to twenty-five, max. No more. What are you smiling about?"

"You know if we tell them twenty to twenty-five, the price is going to be twenty-five."

"Yes. Okay. Twenty-five, max, not a penny more. We want to start building June first. Tell them we want a beautiful kitchen and an enjoyable construction period."

" 'Enjoyable construction period.' Tom. So succinct. I'll call. See who's available, amenable, who sounds nice. Maybe evenings this week or next Saturday."

"Good. Have them bring references and portfolios and ask them to tell us how they'd go about working with us . . . and ask them about their fee. What do I do?" Tom said.

"Prepare the tag sale."

Chris Layner drove through the Finleys' neighborhood slowly, looking for their address. Again, she glanced in her rearview mirror, stopped in the middle of the street, and took a good look at another house. Like most of the houses in the neighborhood, it was built in the twenties before the stock market crash. Nothing incredibly fancy but like the rest, very well detailed. This house, a Tudor variation with a nice round portico, was the work of the same architect who did the other Tudors in the neighborhood. So far, she could pick out the work of three distinct architects within a half-mile radius. Neighborhoods usually built up that way, and now, as Chris saw it, it was time for another architect to move into practice here.

Most of the houses looked like they were very well maintained but not updated since the sixties. Similar houses in the same neighborhood tend to age at the same rate. A wave of residents and children would move into a neighborhood and they would stay until their children moved to college. Then almost all at once, all the old families would sell and a new wave would come in, renovating as they came. This looked like a neighborhood just turning over its housing stock, with a few houses already being renovated. They needed an architect to work these renovations to keep the houses looking good and the overall area reflecting the quality that was originally built here.

Chris needed a "neighborhood" to work in. A place that trusted her and kept her busy. Until now, she had had a hard time finding her niche. After graduating from architecture school she'd been determined to design unusual, iconoclastic buildings. The realities of architecture had done battle with her, though, and now she found most of her income coming from contractors who paid her to draw up their boxy additions for the building department. These additions usually made no sense to her from a design perspective; they were just expansions of the footprint of the house. The additions often sported different details from the rest of the house—plain baseboard, slab doors rather than raised panel, mismatched siding—and they rarely fit into the life of the house in any integral way.

Unfortunately, Chris never got to meet the clients. She was just the draftsperson for the contractor. Someone the contractor knew who would draw up the plans for a reasonable fee.

She did have a small practice as well. The Jacksons, who had referred her to the Finleys, were clients. These commissioned works were much more interesting, but there were problems, especially before she figured out a few things.

In the problem jobs, she'd often ended up with some horrible contractor who hated her designs and did everything he could to convince the owners that the architect was an idiot. The truth is her early designs were often good in theory but weren't expressed very well on paper. She was embarrassed at her ignorance, but rather than ask the contractor his advice, Chris drew the plans as she guessed the project should be built. This was worse because now the contractor had her ignorance in writing and he would usually run straight to the owner.

Chris also had some horrible clients, ones who kept changing their minds, letting her build something her way, then rejecting it and having the whole thing torn apart and reassembled in a way they felt would be better (which rarely satisfied them either). Then they would all get into an argument over who should pay for the changes.

Chris was mystified by two things: why the contractors kept criticizing her, when she got them the job; and why her owners kept changing their minds.

Finally, Chris talked to her mother, a fabric designer, who put an unusual spin on the whole problem. She said it is imperative to respect people, whether clients or contractors. Not simply to say you respect them, but to keep looking for the good in their character and taste. Until you find the things to respect about them, nothing will work right.

Chris thought that over and realized that in order to establish "control" or "authority," she had been treating the contractor and his workers as "the help." She thought of them as laborers working for a more educated client and architect. Chris now saw that they were taking every opportunity to give her a knocking by showing her as an incompetent architect.

Chris also realized that she wasn't taking her design from the owners' cues. She was ignoring their tastes and lobbying for designs that she thought were appropriate. She would work to convince them of her superior taste, claiming that they weren't "seeing" it in the plans but that once it was built, they would be able to appreciate it. Finally, the owners would agree to build her plans, but when they saw the new spaces, the same objections resurfaced.

Respect. Listen. Act. These were Chris's new buzzwords, and with the last three clients, things had improved. Many of her design ideas were inspired by the clients' interviews. She'd asked many questions about the intended use of the space and she took a hard look at what the original architect had done with the house. At first, Chris feared that she was subjugating her own design sense to the other parties—the owner, the previous architect, the neighborhood. But she found herself putting more of her personality into the building as she struggled to find a design that satisfied and sprang from these different inspirations.

The Finley's house.

Chris stopped in the middle of the street and looked at the house. It had a nice gabled roof. Freshly painted. Neat without being obsessively fastidious. Great massing. It was heavy, solid, rooted. She could find a lot to like in this house.

"So," Michelle said, sizing up the new architect, "what do you think of the kitchen?"

Chris said quickly, "It's really quite horrible, isn't it? If the rest of the house wasn't so nice, I'd be afraid to say that for fear this was your doing, too."

Tom visibly relaxed. "It's true. The rest of the house we love—we just knew this room was going to cost us some serious money and we've been slow in getting to it."

"I can understand that," Chris said, thinking of her own atrocious kitchen, which looked nearly as bad. "I'm afraid there isn't much to save here."

"So looking at the space, do you have any ideas?" Tom said.

Chris smiled a queer smile. "I don't know how much the Jacksons told you about me, but I'm rather slow. I used to be fast—I designed precisely what I liked, which came to me quite quickly. Then the rest of the design process was taken up trying to convince the poor people that my design was what they wanted. Now I purposely don't imagine what the project should look like. I ask questions and I take a good look at what you like. Once that work is done, I try to use you as an inspiration and design something that I like."

Michelle nodded. "But without hearing your ideas, why should we hire you? I mean, what can we go on?"

"I've brought my portfolio and some letters from the clients I've worked this way with. I've also brought a questionnaire you can fill out. It'll get us started if we decide to work together. Believe me, it would be much easier to get the job if I spun out some ideas right now, but then we'd be hobbling along with those ideas for the rest of the project."

Tom and Michelle looked at each other. Chris was the fourth and final architect they'd met with. All three of the others had given loads of concepts about what they should do with their kitchen. They were getting green curtains, brass doorknobs, flowerpots, and three different Viking ranges. It had been very impressive that these architects and designers could design so quickly, and with each of them the Finleys had been excited. However, by the next morning the Finleys had sincere doubts about the different concepts. In addition, each architect had left the Finleys feeling somehow outside of the process. What Ms. Layner was proposing sounded more involved but more interesting as well.

"Could we take a look at your portfolio?" Tom said.

Everybody was standing in the kitchen, looking dejectedly at a hole in the wall. Giovanni DeTomaso's son Leonardo was the only one covered in dust—everyone else was just staring at the swirling particles as they blew around the just-revealed heavy timber going up to the second floor.

"So why didn't we know before that this column was going to be here?" Tom Finley asked, a distinct edge in his voice.

Giovanni DeTomaso instantly answered in kind. "Mr. Finley, for six hundred dollars I go down to the building department, I research your house, I scale off the old plans. I come here, I tell you I don't know anything for sure but maybe this, maybe that. This way, for two hundred fifty dollars, Leonardo comes with the hammer—boom boom, we know for sure."

Finley wasn't stopping. "But you're professionals—"

Chris Layner interjected. "It's not Mr. DeTomaso's fault that there's a column here, and he's right. The work done to a house is rarely documented, and even if it is, it's rarely documented well."

"But this destroys the whole design. How can we have a dining room with a beam, or column, or whatever the hell it is right in the middle of it?" Tom Finley was angry.

His wife's voice was quick: "Tom, would you rather we had found out about this after all the final blueprints were drawn, we had started demolition, and all the cabinets were sitting in the garage?"

"No, I would rather that this damn *column* weren't here!"

"Go get the Sawzall, Leonardo," Giovanni said.

Everyone looked at Giovanni.

"You want the column out, we cut the column out. If she falls on our head, we know why it's there."

Tom's mood changed quickly. "No, Mr. DeTomaso, if it has to be there . . ."

"No, we take it out. You don't like it, I'm here to please, we take it out."

Leonardo was already out the door to their truck.

"Mr. DeTomaso, there must be another way—"

"To get rid of the column? To pretend it's not there holding up the second floor? No . . . Good, Leonardo, plug this in over there."

The Sawzall had a twelve-inch coarse cutting blade, and as Leonardo plugged it in, the blade sang to life.

"There's got to be another way," Tom Finley said.

"You want to yell and scream," DeTomaso said, "then this is the only way. You want to ask us as professionals"—DeTomaso indicated Chris Layner and himself—"then maybe we find a way around your problem. You tell me."

Tom Finley's face turned bright red. "I apologize."

There was a pause as DeTomaso let it sink in, then shrugged his shoulders. "I understand," he said. "You're upset we have a column where we don't want a column. This is a little problem now. If we didn't find this out today—if we wait until demolition and I knock down this whole wall and then find the column—we are stuck. We lose time while we consult engineer; the cabinets we put on hold, will delay my crew. Now it's just annoying. So what are we going to do, Ms. Layner?"

Chris Layner was barely controlling her smile. She had never heard of Mr. DeTomaso but she was very impressed. This was a man with money in the bank. "Well, I imagine we could either build some kind of header inside a soffit—perhaps place it over the center island—or we could drop cabinets from the ceiling and hide the header in the cabinets; or we could bring one set of cabinets up from the center island and make them structural; or maybe patch the hole, leave the den where it is, and build the kitchen out the other direction."

"Very good, Ms. Layner," DeTomaso said, moving in the direction of the kitchen's other wall. "She's quite smart, this designer. Quite smart. Maybe we open a little hole in this wall now?"

Design Checklist

Money

- Decide how much money you have to spend and plan a budget. Consider factors such as surrounding property values and the length of time you expect to live there before you decide on a spending plan.
- Use quality architects, designers, and contractors to get the most out of your budget.
- Tell the budget to everyone.
- Let contractors compete on what they can give you for that budget.
- Find a qualified architect to guide you through the design.
- Pay a contractor to consult on the plans, probe existing conditions, and give alternate prices as you design.
- Make your job a "trophy project" that gives architects and contractors benefits beyond their profit (e.g., job contacts, great photos, publicity).

Time

- Develop a time line for the design phase of your project ending in a "bid set" of drawings and hand it out to prospective architects and contractors.
- Stick to that time line and don't be pressured out of it.
- Schedule meetings and deadlines precisely and confirm them the day before. Arrive on time for all meetings.

Power

- Build a team by establishing the roles of architect, contractor, and owner.
- Establish the shared goal; a beautiful project, on time and on budget.

- Hire the architect and contractor through recommendations from past clients, lumberyards, and professional organizations so that they have secondary reasons for dealing with you professionally.

Management
- Buy this book for everyone involved in your project.
- Watch for management problems that may arise in any of the three of you and take quick steps to correct them.
- Use my money-based decision analysis method to make decisions, assigning dollar values to utility and aesthetic concerns.
- Use the contractor for objective criticism during construction.

Quality
- Choose a designer or architect, as well as a contractor, whose capabilities are appropriate for your job.
- Use the checklist in this section when checking references.
- Make it clear to everyone that you want the best quality of design and execution.
- Control price with expense of materials and intricacy of design rather than with the quality of execution.
- Be clear about what you expect from bids and proposals.
- Don't try to make design decisions before you or your design professional is ready.

Part Two

Contracting

1

The Hamptons—
Making a Contract
with the Devil

Karen was walking stiffly up the driveway, the newest plans under her arm. She passed Larry and Cindy's Pathfinder and she felt like kicking it. They had a $22,000 four-wheel drive to impress the boys at the gas station but couldn't afford to pay her $750 to do a plan. "But we're your friends," Larry and Cindy had said.

"Then why are you stealing two hundred and fifty dollars?" Karen felt like saying back.

The disgusting thing was that the only reason Karen had bothered to design the plans again was that she needed the $500. She knew she wouldn't make any money—but then she hadn't made any money on interior design in years. She was just trying to keep ahead of the taxman.

Karen rang the doorbell and the first three notes of "The Blue Danube" waltz played.

Nothing.

Karen waited. No sound from inside the house. Karen rang again. "Duh duh duh." The first three notes of "The Blue Danube" are the same—a tough song for *Name That Tune*, but Karen recognized it because the doorbell used to play the whole first bar. Karen glanced at her watch. She was on time. She had risked a speeding ticket to get there on time. She glanced in the garage but couldn't tell whether Cindy's car was inside.

She heard the sound of a pickup coming down the street. It was Prime Construction. Great. Now she was going to be waiting with a contractor. Waiting for Cindy. Cindy had wanted Prime to look at the new plans at the same time she did so they could start getting some prices as soon as possible. Karen had told her it would be better to wait until she and Larry had gone through the drawings, but Cindy had insisted that since Prime's bids were free, they should bid now, and if Larry had to change some things later, so be it.

The pickup swerved into the driveway and a thick head popped out. "Is she here?"

"Uh, Mrs. Hampton?"

"Yeah. She was late half an hour the first time I gave her a bid. Is she here?"

"I'm afraid she's a little late."

Without another word, the Prime Construction truck ground into reverse, swerved back into the road, and vanished.

Larry Hampton was looking at the plans without touching them. He was even sitting slightly sideways in his chair as he looked at them, as though he didn't want to commit himself. Cindy was inspecting the plans carefully, and Karen was doing her best to look perky and fresh, even though this was her third attempt to deliver the set of plans. Cindy had never shown up on Tuesday, rescheduled it for Wednesday, and then called that off after Karen had moved all her other appointments around. Finally, she had rescheduled the appointment for Sunday morning.

"I can't tell from this," Larry said. "Are we using the cabinets we already have?"

"Yes."

"Do we have to buy any more?"

"No more cabinets. I've made up the extra area with simple open shelving units."

"Well, how's that going to look?" Larry asked, doubting.

Karen's veneer slipped away. "Listen, if you want me to use your cabinets and not buy any more, I'm going to have to do something to make up the missing dimensions."

"Karen," Cindy said, "Larry was just asking how it would look. There's no reason to be defensive."

"Sorry," Karen said. "It's just that this is the fourth time I've tried to present plans."

"Four? Two," Larry said.

"What do you mean four times, Karen?"

"Well, there were the original plans."

"One." Cindy smiled.

"Then I came on Tuesday—"

"Oh, I'm sorry about that."

"Then we had it scheduled for Wednesday."

"But I called and canceled that."

"But I still had it in my schedule."

"You mean you just sat at home while we were supposed to be having our meeting? No, you did something else. You've presented two sets of plans. And we appreciate that. Larry, what do you think about these?"

"What did Prime Construction's price come in at?"

Karen was barely holding her temper. "Prime Construction is not bidding. They came on Tuesday, and when Cindy wasn't here, they left."

"Call them back. This is work," Larry said. "How about that thief? Has he looked at the plans yet?"

"No, I wanted you to look at them first to see if there were any changes."

"Karen," Cindy said, "time is slipping away. What are you waiting for?"

"We were supposed to meet on Tuesday. Now it's Sunday. I didn't reschedule that."

Larry shook his head. "Listen, the plans are basically fine, I'm sure. Karen, if you could get them to a few contractors. We'll look them over and call you if we have any big problems. Can we keep this set?"

Karen watched the plans slide across the table. She could tell she wasn't getting paid.

Henry Jorgensen, contractor, was looking at his desk for a place to spread out these new plans. He laid them out carefully on top of what was there—a good four inches above what was once the surface of the desk. Henry's basic take on bookwork was that the only things that were important had red writing on the outside of the envelope. All other things got put on his desk. Disconnect notices, eviction notices, audit notices; those got his attention every time and he'd find his checkbook and stop them for a little while. Otherwise, he put it on the desk.

A big dictionary came dislodged and slid across the faces of some magazines and off the desktop, barely missing his bruised toes. Henry never wore work shoes and he kept dropping tools and sheets of Masonite on his toes lately. Henry left the dictionary there and unfolded the cover page of the drawings. God, he hated drawings. Henry just liked to get in there and build. He was the fastest guy up a ladder, but this bookwork stuff drove him crazy. He liked action, not trying to figure out where $4.67 had vanished. The way things always worked was he got on the job, the architect explained to him what she wanted, and Henry worked his own way to that goal. He never knew how much to bid, though. He would kind of look at the plans, figure out how many weeks it would take, throw in some money for materials, and add something for his trouble.

A cat jumped up on the drawings and his wet pawprints left muddy streaks just where Henry was looking. Henry swept aside the cat, who collided with a stack of old *Weekend Woodworker*s and knocked the whole pile to the floor.

"Fifteen thousand dollars? Where did he get fifteen thousand dollars?" Cindy asked.

Karen had come over with the first bid from Henry Jorgensen. She had a number from Frank and the new number from Prime, too. Before Karen had answered, Larry spoke:

"Karen, we hired you because a contractor gave us a bid for two thousand dollars to screw some cabinets up to the wall. We thought you'd save us money. Now we've paid you five hundred dollars and the contractor's price is fifteen thousand."

"Henry Jorgensen is a very careful and meticulous man, but believe me, he overbids. I'm sure he can come down. You have to remember that there is a lot more in these plans than just screwing some cabinets up. We're knocking down walls, we're putting in new floors, new counters, new electric, and moving plumbing. That's a lot of trades trooping through your house."

"What's Prime Construction now?" Larry asked.

"They're thirty."

"FOR THE SAME WORK?"

"Prime doesn't want the job. I got a price from your friend Frank. He's up to six thousand seven hundred."

Karen got up and looked at the cabinets in the dining room. "This seems crazy. What do we decide?"

Larry started to laugh. "Frank. Definitely Frank. See, we found that guy. But tell him his price is still high. Get him down to five. I bet he'll go. Tell him we'll give him the job for five thousand. What's the worst that can happen?"

"Have you looked at his work?" Karen asked.

"He's fine."

"Can he take down this wall?"

"Sure, he's a contractor. He'll be fine. He's just not a thief like the rest. So, Karen, what do we do next?"

"I just want to say that it seems strange he's so low. If you want to go ahead with him, I can draw up a contract, file for permits, do some more drawings."

"And charge us another five hundred dollars. No thank you, Karen."

"Larry!"

"Cindy, we're going with a contractor we found originally, for more than twice the money. I'm not going to pay her a thousand dollars for her contributions."

Karen's hands were shaking as they gripped hold of the copy of the plans that Larry was holding and she tried to pull them away. "Give it. Just give it. Don't pay me. Just give me back my plans." With a mighty yank, the plans gave way and Karen stomped out of the house, tears welling up but not streaming down her face until she was pulling out of the driveway.

"Frank'll still have a set of those drawings, right?" Larry asked as they watched Karen's little car chug off down the road.

Cindy dialed the phone, a piece of paper in front of her, Larry off to her side. "Hello, Frank? . . . Yes, this is Cindy Hampton . . . Yes. Listen, we got your price from Karen; frankly we were a little shocked by how much it had gone up." Cindy listened for a minute, idly printing "$5,000" on the paper for Larry to see.

"Well, since you were the first person to be recommended to us, we really wanted to use you. It's just . . . Frankly, your price is high."

Larry took Cindy's pen from her hand and wrote on the paper: "Ask him what's included."

Cindy snapped her fingers quietly to get the pen back. "Uhh-huhh . . . Yes, I know the plans got more specific. What's in your price now?"

"Demolition," Cindy wrote down on the paper as Frank talked. "Materials, construction—"

Larry shook his head vigorously, snatched the pen back, and wrote, "What work is he doing for the money? Floors? Counters?"

Cindy took the pen back again. "Are you doing all the work in the plans?" She nodded at Larry. "Well, I just don't see how that adds up to sixty-seven hundred . . . The other contractors? Frank, I can't tell you that. That would be a breach of ethics. You just tell me your best price . . ."

"You'll *split* the difference? Hmm." Cindy put a slash through the $5,000. "We were at two thousand, then you said sixty-seven hundred. Shall we just say forty-three hundred and be done with it?"

There was a pause. Cindy wrote down "$4,000" on the paper.

"Five thousand? Frank, you suggested splitting it . . . I don't know . . . Forty-eight twenty-five? . . . How about forty-five? . . . Okay, hold on." Cindy covered the mouthpiece. "Forty-five hundred instead of Jorgensen's fifteen?"

Larry nodded.

"How soon could you get us a contract? . . . Yes, you write something up . . . And when could you start? . . . A down payment? What kind of down payment? . . . All right. If you start Thursday. Very good. I'll call you back."

Cindy put down the phone. She had the look in her eyes that Larry first fell in love with.

2

Money
Problems

There are two kinds of weekend woodworkers. Both want to build a bookcase. The first draws out in exact detail how he will build a set of bookcases. This drawing shows every dimension and how the pieces of wood fit together. He even goes back and recalculates the dimensional totals just to make sure there's been no mistake. His drawing exactly represents all the carpentry. Once that drawing is made, actually cutting and putting the bookcase together is a fait accompli.

Likewise, during the design phase of your renovation project you will have worked the design completely through, but because you're not doing the work yourself, you now need to define your relationship with the contractor just as carefully. Once this carefully detailed contract has been added to your blueprint, you have in your hand a complete representation of your renovation project. Now the crews need only begin the work.

The other weekend woodworker will be eager to start working and he'll make very sketchy drawings. The drawing will be enough to cut the first piece of wood and then measure off of that to cut the second piece of wood. At about the fourth piece he'll realize that it would have been better if the first piece was three-quarters of an inch wider so that he could join it to the fifth piece, but instead of cutting a new first piece, he makes the fifth piece a little wider to compensate. When he gets to the eighth piece, he'll realize that the first piece really does have to be three-quarters of an inch wider, so he'll make a new first piece and shave three-quarters off the fifth piece. Then he'll realize that he cut three-quarters off the width instead of the length of the fifth piece.

A relationship with a contractor based on that model will perform just the same. It may be quicker to get going, but by the fifth piece, you'll be in trouble.

Deciding on the final contract price is a milestone for everyone. Up until now, owners have been dealing with money in the abstract: what they think they can afford; how much their likely promotion will bring them. How much the taxes on an inheritance might be. Suddenly, the contract is upon them and it's time to inspect the bank account and see what's actually there. Throughout the design phase, discussions of money have been hypothetical; owner, architect, and contractor have moved thousands of dollars without batting an eye. Now it's time to make a deal.

From the architect's point of view, the final contract price is her opportunity to prove she's worth her money. By bringing down the contractor's price as much as possible she will be able to "pay for herself." Ask anyone in sales what's easy to sell and it's the service that "pays for itself." The architect wants to show that thanks to her services, the owner will come out better financially.

For the contractor, money is much more volatile. The designer's fee is based on an hourly rate. There are few unknowns there. But the contractor is agreeing to build everything on the drawings for a set price. There's no way to know how long it's going to take to put a door in, much less install custom-made stainless-steel shutters. Yet contractors have to make these estimations. If they underestimate the time it will take or forget some part of a job, they may not make a cent on your project.

But the contractor is faced with considerable pressure from the architect to underestimate.

This brings up a curious phenomenon about money. People value money less as the amounts get larger. Most people will not go into a butcher and pay $18 a pound for filet mignon. It's just too much money, they can't afford it. But if they're paying for a $40,000 renovation, $600 in final negotiations is no big deal.

When we step back, though, we see that $600 is almost thirty-three times as much money as the filet mignon. Their point of reference for what is expensive has shifted from dollars to thousands of dollars even though the value of money has not changed. It's easy to get careless this way.

A contractor is struck down by the same sword. If he's getting ready to do a $40,000 job and realizes he forgot to include a $250 item, he's not likely to bring it up. But in reality, of that $40,000, only $3,000 or $4,000 will end up in his bank account at the end as profit. Rather than comparing that $250 to the $40,000, the contractor should be comparing $250 to $4,000. The $250 represents $1/16$ of his profit, not $1/160$ of the total job.

The Hamptons are falling into bigger problems. First, they are allowing themselves the fantasy that Frank is a miracle worker who can do their job for thousands of dollars less than another bidder.

It's true, somewhere in America there is the old carpenter we talked about before who owns his own home, has no children to put through college, isn't married, and has a bad self-image but a great talent with tools. He is organized, he has materials he bought twenty years ago in bulk that cost him nothing to use today, and he can charge half of what everyone else charges. This man exists, and every year tens of thousands of homeowners create headaches for themselves by thinking they've hired him. Somewhere he exists, but it's very unlikely he lives in your town or that he's available for work.

Instead you'll get someone who pretends he's him and the price that contractor gives will be 25 percent lower than everyone else, but the quality and performance will be half of what you require. When you get a very low price, there is a .5 percent chance that you've found some Maine craftsman who's going to do a great job for a low price. But you have a 99.5 percent chance of getting burned, of wasting money, of doing work to your house that will have to be done over by the next tenants.

Why do you think Frank can deliver a bid (even before negotiation) that's $8,000 less than his competition? Frank's not a crook but he is incompetent and he's blinded by need—quite probably because his short-term self-preservation relies on it. Frank has a big bill with the IRS and he's afraid of the consequences if he doesn't pay. When an opportunity comes to get some money to hand to the IRS, the self-preserving part of Frank's brain overrides all of his other systems and tells him to get that money at all costs.

Frank will go on to cross his fingers, not make a materials list, and hope for the best.

Frank is "forgetting" that knocking down a wall is not just hitting it with a hammer and throwing it in the truck. It means: protecting the floor and the rest of the house from dust; carefully marking out the wall for cutting; constructing some sort of temporary support for the ceiling so that it doesn't collapse while the work is being done; inserting some kind of reinforcement into the joists to hold up the second floor; hauling the construction debris away; and finishing the reinforcement to the joists in an attractive way.

Everyone else's bids will include this part of the work, for perhaps $4,000. Frank will bid $1,250 because he's just planning on knocking out the wall and throwing it in the truck; plus profit. The owners don't see anything wrong with the price because they want to spend the least amount of money. To them, the extra $2,750 seems like pure thievery.

The Hamptons' second mistake is not paying the designer. Imagine if you will that you were taking a vacation in the heart of some exotic country when tribal infighting suddenly erupts and there is widespread bloodshed. Frantically, you search for a guide to get you out. Luckily, you find such a guide and you make an agreement, you will pay him $200 today, $200 in three days, and $1,000 when you are out of the country and at a free airport. So you pay the guide $200, he has you crawling down creek beds and staying in trees at night. After three days you haven't seen the airport yet and the next payment is due. You get nervous, so you say, "Hey, guide, I'm not paying you the next two hundred until you get us to the airport. Then I'll give you the whole twelve hundred."

Now, there is a 25 percent chance that your fears are justified; that the guide isn't planning on getting you out, that he's going to take your second $200 and turn you over to the tribal infighting on the other side of the hedgerow.

There is a 75 percent chance that he's on the up-and-up, wants to get the hell out himself and make the $1,400 to boot. Let's also face facts: right now he is your only hope of avoiding death.

At the same time, stiffing him for that second payment has a 100 percent chance of making him angry and a 100 percent chance of making him think that once he delivers you to safety, you're going to stiff him then, too. You have proved yourself untrustworthy.

By speaking this sentence, "Hey, guide, I'm not paying you the next $200 until . . ." you have radically changed the game. There is now a 75 percent chance that the guide will cease risking his life to get you to safety. If he stays your guide, his heart will no longer be in it because he is afraid that you are going to stiff him and he doesn't want to end up being the dupe. Instead, he may leave you here, $200 richer, and either go find someone else to save or just leave the guide business altogether.

Yet every day, architects tell me that clients aren't paying them on time. Architects are guides—that is effectively their business— and it is important to treat your guide well.

3

Solutions to
Money Problems

F *lash! Thieving contractors never come in with the highest bid!*

However, it's not necessary to take the highest bid. What you're looking for is the *best* bid; and the best bid will include prices for everything you want done as well as prices for things you need to have but didn't know to request. In order to install new tile, what you didn't think of was installing a new subfloor. In order to build a shed, you also need a city permit.

It's therefore essential that the bid be broken down into all the bits of work to be done. Most contractors don't like to do that for two reasons:

1. They haven't done it themselves and they don't want to admit that they're just guessing.

2. They are rightfully afraid that if they write down on paper that it costs $350 to put in a new door, you're going to say that you've been to the Home Depot and you've seen complete doors there for $65 including hinges and brass knob. Instead, they'd rather cloak everything in mystery and just give you a grand total. Then you'll be less likely to fixate on individual items to try to talk them down.

However, it's important for you to know why your project costs as much as it does. Say, for instance, you cavalierly decide to retile the bathroom floor as long as you're changing the toilet. Finding that it costs $750 to tile the bathroom floor may prompt you to think about carpet instead.

Likewise, comparing the various parts of different bids will show you that while one contractor is charging you $250 for retiling the bathroom floor, everyone else is charging $750. Maybe the first contractor likes you? Or perhaps you've found the old bachelor craftsman? More likely, someone is planning to use Fixodent to set the tiles. In any event, something is wrong with the picture. Either the first contractor doesn't understand the scope of the job, or nobody else does.

You shouldn't try shopping prices around to the different bidders because this will only annoy the contractors. Instead, try shopping quality. "This other contractor is offering a solid mahogany front door. Could you do that?"

Never let anyone know that his bid is lowest. From that point on, the contractor will be kicking himself in the backside for not charging more, will be charging you for every possible extra he can dream of to make up some ground, and will have a bad attitude about the work in general. Tell a contractor you are choosing him despite the fact that he is a little higher than everyone else, because you think he has a better understanding of the project and will produce better quality. The contractor may not completely believe you, but in his heart of hearts, he'll be happy to pretend to.

What if the man you want to hire really is the most expensive? A good technique is to say, "Look, I really want to hire you. You're obviously the best, but my budget is set at ten thousand, and I can't go above that. How can you help me get to that?" He should make suggestions of ways to simplify or adjust parts of the work so that it's possible. If he won't, he may be too busy, thinks he's the lowest price, or isn't very creative.

In order to get a lower price, you'll have little luck yelling across the fence, "Charge less," while he yells back, "Pay more." You have to expand the negotiation to include other items of value; to make the negotiation "asymmetrical," rather than rigidly squared off over a single issue. In short, there are many different "bargaining chips" you can use. You can change the scope of work, change the time frame that the work has to be done by, offer that the owner does some of the work, offer that the contractor will do some extra work for the same money, offer that the owner will work to get the contractor more jobs, etc.

Say, for instance, that you're doing substantial renovations to an existing design studio which happens to be located in the center of a small town. Following the renovation, this little building will be one of the most striking features of the town. Yes, price will be important to the contractor, but the notoriety of the building can be made important as well. Contractors, as we all remember, have to keep getting new jobs, and therefore they are constantly spending money on advertising to get those new jobs. An agreement to install a plaque on the corner of the building, listing the builder, architect, and client, is a definite side bonus. This could be especially effective if you put it into context for the contractor: that *some* contractor will get on the plaque and you hope it's them. They may scoff at it, but it's worth a try.

What you don't want is for the contractor to just come down in price without getting anything in return. He'll feel cheated and taken advantage of and he'll most likely resent you. You need to give him something so he can go back to his partner and say, "Look, we're going to have to go down a thousand dollars, but in return, besides her unending thanks, she's willing to invite us to the housewarming party and leave a bowl of our cards out on a table. She's also agreeing to give us unlimited access to show her apartment to people during the upcoming two years and she's offered to bring by two pizzas and two sixes of Coke every Friday during the job." It may sound preposterous, but for people sitting on the fence these kinds of offers are going to make contractors more likely to say yes. Add an extra month to the construction schedule and you may have a deal.

If the contractor can't come down on his price, try to arrange for him to throw in some extra bonuses. You might ask for a speedy completion, a completely clean job site every Friday night, professional cleaning at the end of the job, or an extended warrantee.

Now that we've got our price, it's time to set up the money as the engine for the project.

The pay schedule has to be fair to both sides. Neither the contractor nor the owner should ever be far ahead of the other; in other words, the contractor shouldn't be walking around with a big deposit while owing the owners work. Nor should the contractor have done a lot of work and be waiting to get paid. In my experience, a down payment should never be above 30 percent. Otherwise, even for the best contractor, there is the feeling that there's no money left in the job and therefore no incentive to get it done.

Once we've determined a down payment, we must progress to a pay schedule. The standard pay schedule has rigid and simple terms. It's usual to pay 30 percent down, 15 percent at frame-up, 15 percent with finished walls, 10 percent at doors, windows, and bucks, 10 percent at painting, and 10 percent at floors, with 10 percent left at the end for retainage. This schedule ignores the reality that the construction process rarely goes strictly by the planner's schedule. What happens when the contractor discovers a structural defect that must be inspected before framing can finish? Does the job stop while everyone waits? Is a partial payment made? Does work continue without payment?

Instead, I recommend a pay schedule that acknowledges that work is frequently held up for unforeseen reasons and that it benefits everyone if other work can be completed in its place. Therefore, what I prefer is a pay schedule tied to the bid breakdown.

My pay schedule is a hybrid and I feel it works very efficiently. This is how it works:

First, I split the total cost of the job into six parts (I'll use a $15,000 job): $15,000 ÷ 6 = $2,500.

I ask clients to make a 15 percent deposit, although depending on the job and client it may vary. I then divide the balance into six equal payments: 15% of $15,000 = $2,250 down, which leaves $12,750 ÷ 6 = $2,125 payments × 6.

As I work, I compare the work I've done to the itemized breakdown, and when I've done work valued at one-sixth of the job ($2,500), I request a payment ($2,125).

Here's a sample pay request:

Work Completed	Value in Itemized Bid
Demo and site prep: completed	**$1,500**
New closet wall: framing completed (50% of total)	250
Closet shelves: completed	175
Electric rough-in: 25% of total completed	400
SUBTOTAL	2,325
Profit and overhead (20%)	465
Total work completed	2,790
⅙ of work	2,500
Amount applied toward next milestone	290
PAYMENT DUE NOW	**$1,750**

Notice that I had to do $2,500 of work to get $1,750. That's because I already took out an advance of 30 percent on the whole job. Incidentally, during the work, we discovered a pipe in the wall that needed to be removed by the plumber, so I've had to hold off putting up the Sheetrock. Instead of just waiting, though, I've gone ahead and put shelves in the closet—something I wasn't planning on doing until the end of the job—but I've rearranged things so that I can get my next payment. As a side bonus, finishing the shelves now, means I've extra time to close up this wall later, keeping me on schedule. In a traditional payment plan, my payment would have been "at completion of walls," and so I would have had to either wait for the plumber or convince the owner to pay me anyway. This way, the mechanism for dealing with the unexpected is built-in, payment is made smoothly and fairly, and workers stay on the job. A 15 percent down payment works well but only if you couple it with a very fast payment method so the contractor doesn't run out of money. You should agree to payment within two days of pay requests.

4

Time Problems

During the design phase, people usually waste time by "digesting" the design or taking too long to consider small details. These periods of inactivity are generally signs of either a failure to commit to the project or a misunderstanding of the importance of details.

It can take days of concentrated effort to read and compare bids, get insurance certificates, read contracts, reprice for changes, look at different tile, get the building permit. Instead, this process can be stretched out to weeks as people consistently fail to devote time to these important, though seemingly mundane and insignificant chores. The project cannot start without all of these details being finalized despite everyone's desire to get moving.

People put these details off either because they fail to recognize their priorities and haven't set aside time to devote to the project or because they are still not sure about the design or the money.

To the architect, this time lag may be welcome. Because she has other jobs going at the same time, she has limited time to devote to resolving all of the final design issues—issues that haven't been resolved yet because for some reason they are difficult by their nature. For her, there's no great push to get the construction started. In fact, the more she can put it off, the more time she has to straighten out the details while still having time for her other projects.

But for the contractor, and consequently for you, this slowdown can be deadly. Until the contracts are signed, the contractor has no money, and no work for his crews. So the contractor and his crews will fill their time in with small jobs.

These small jobs will be extremely detrimental to your project, but they're necessary for the contractor to preserve himself. As these filler jobs ebb and flow, the contractor will alternately push for an immediate start date, then drag his heels to slow the process down.

It is also necessary for the contractor to hedge his bets by bidding on several projects at the same time. A contractor is constantly getting offers of work, and until he has a commitment, he must keep each going until he's signed a contract. Unfortunately, by the time he gets word that he has the job he wants, he may have strung the others along so far that he feels he can't say no to them either. Finally, like a character in a painful sitcom, he accepts all the jobs and tries vainly to keep it a secret from the others. He dances back and forth between them all until the whole charade finally falls apart.

5

Solutions to Time Problems

Contractors adjust their prices depending on how much work they have. If they're too busy, they know their efficiency goes down, because rather than being able to swing a hammer themselves to do the complicated parts that only they understand, they'll have to hire a very smart and expensive carpenter and explain it to him. I have a client with a loft bed who needed a way of folding the ladder during the day. If I do it myself, it will take me an hour to fabricate the mechanism at the shop and another hour to install it. If I charge $300, $100 will go to overhead and expenses and I'll happily make $100 an hour. The owner will be happy, too, because I've solved his ladder problem.

However, if I'm too busy to do it, I'll have to hire somebody else. This person will cost me, in New York City, $250 a day. I'll have him meet me at the shop, I'll make a shop drawing and have him fabricate it. Then I have to get him to the site, show him where and how to install it. I'll keep this guy busy for a day, provided he gets it right the first time, and I'll put at least an hour into it myself. If I add in overhead of $100, I'm going to have to charge $500 and I'll still make less money. Now picture hiring a contractor for a whole renovation and think of the extra amount he'll have to charge if he's too busy to do it himself. It pays to look around to find the good contractor who's not busy. Most good contractors *are* busy, so at least contact them enough in advance that they can make room for you. A great contractor who's too busy is of no use to you.

During the design period the constraints on time tended to be loose as you thought about the various options. During the contracting phase you need to project a new image of yourself as very time-conscious. You need to set a deadline for all bids and make it clear to the bidding contractors that you will be judging them by whether they can meet the deadline. Make it specific: 5:00 P.M. on Friday, 11:30 Monday morning. Make it clear that you will not accept any bids after the specified time and then don't accept them. If they can't honor this deadline, they're not going to have the systems in place to honor your later deadlines.

This may seem very harsh, but if you want to get the job on time, you need to show how serious you are about time. Imposing strict deadlines on your contractor will allow him to impose strict deadlines on you. He won't feel bad asking you to decide the color of the kitchen by Friday.

Let everyone know that there's going to be a strict time schedule on the job and that for any proposed changes, the cost must be given beforehand in terms of extra money and time required.

Now the tricky part. Deadlines in contracts must have teeth or contractors will have no reason to meet them. However, if you impose a penalty for lateness, you'll have to give a bonus for early completion or it will be considered unfair by your contractor, which is not a good way to start this relationship. You are in control of the management of your project, but it is a three-way partnership.

To make a penalty clause work, your bid request must require a schedule for the work as well as the price. Make it clear that the bids will be competing on time as well as money, but that their schedule must be realistic.

You may find that contractors with shorter construction schedules are more expensive because they'll bring in larger crews. You'll have to decide if a shorter construction period is worth the extra money. If you are carrying two mortgages or rental payments until you can move into your new house, time bears a strict relationship to money. If you're living with your parents during the work, you may not be as concerned about time but very sensitive to cost.

Making time schedules part of the bidding process, though, will ensure that contractors won't inflate their estimated time so that they'll finish early and make a few extra dollars off you.

Once you have a realistic idea of how long the job will take, then you may say:

"So this is a realistic time?"

"Oh yes," the contractor will say.

"You're completely confident?"

"Oh yes."

"So as long as you're certain, let me propose this. We'll have a two-week grace period around that date. If you're more than a week early, I'll pay you twenty-five a day. If you're more than a week late, you'll pay me twenty-five a day. Fair?"

"What happens if you change things?"

"Then when you give me a price for the change, you tell me how long it will take as well."

Contractors don't like penalty clauses for completion dates, but when you're paying them a premium to finish early, it certainly makes it more fair. You're also using the date of completion that the contractor furnished, so you're being fair again. You've also made a provision for changes—and incidentally a reason for you *not* to make changes because the contractor will have an opportunity to increase the contract time whenever you suggest a change.

It's been my experience that when there's been a penalty clause on the construction deadline, I've always completed the job on time.

It's not that I was so afraid of the penalty, it's just that as I made the thousand decisions of a particular job, that penalty clause kept that deadline in the front of my mind.

Likewise, I've used bonuses and penalties on my subcontractors as well. People work damn hard where there's a tangible reward. A marble subcontractor who consistently delivered his countertops two weeks late showed up a week early to collect a bonus $50. Back in the days when he was two weeks late, I wasted much more than $50 bringing plumbers back and standing around with carpenters. I paid that $50 very cheerfully.

Finally, find out from your architect how difficult and how long it takes to get plans approved in your city. Then budget your time accordingly and don't allow your plans to be sent in late. Once they are in the hands of the city government, follow up on them so you'll have the approvals when you're ready to start construction. Otherwise, you'll have done all your work but you won't be allowed to break ground.

6

Power
Problems

We've discussed how important it is that people feel confident in order to negotiate in good faith. Knowledge is essential for confidence, and most owners know they don't fully understand contractual matters. Because their risk is so great (their life's savings), owners are likely to have adverse reactions to signing on the dotted line.

It's not that they don't understand the words of the contract, it's that they fear they are going to make some horrible mistake and be swindled. In a way, it's like a pair of innocent kindergarten teachers from Vermont contemplating going to Atlantic City for the first time to play poker. They can rely on Hoyle's rules, but they know that if the boys from Atlantic City decide to cheat, there is little they can do to stop them.

So, to deal with this powerlessness, owners search out either the most trustworthy contractor or the most stupid and desperate. The owners who look for the stupid contractor believe that by finding a "stupid and desperate" contractor, they won't be powerless. They'll be able to go into the contract and connive, convince, and force the contractor into giving them an amazing deal. Ironically, they usually get an amazing deal.

However, they now have a stupid, desperate contractor at the helm.

The "stupid" contractor, due to his self-preserving ineptness, will probably not draw up a very detailed contract. He will agree to unde-fined work for a low price with many assurances that he will "take care of" whatever things the owners are concerned about. At this point, the owners feel that they are protected because the contractor is stupid and desperate. He has to do a good job.

However, it's amazing how putting a big hole in someone's living room wall can confer intelligence on even the stupidest contractor. These are the steps:

1. Big hole knocked in living room wall.

2. Column discovered within wall that must be moved.

3. Contractor wants an additional $4,000 to move it.

4. Owner refuses.

5. Contractor tells owner to find another contractor.

6. Owner pays big extra and wonders why contractor is no longer stupid or desperate.

The second problem with hiring stupid and desperate contractors is that they know architects aren't going to recommend them. As a result, the architect holds no power of future work over the contrac-tor. The low-priced man always knows there will be work for him, so he can screw up job after job, ask for big extras again and again, because he knows that there is a certain percentage of people in this world who believe that the cheapest price is always the best deal.

The architect allows the owner to accept the lowest bid because she's caught in a difficult situation. The architect is supposed to be the trusted and ethical adviser to the owner. At the same time, her fee is a percentage of the construction cost. Therefore, if the architect argues too vehemently for the more expensive contractor, she can be accused of wanting him in order to inflate her fee.

Ironically, architects should get more when the contractors underbid. Architects have to spend an immense amount of time on the job when the contractor is inept and disorganized. On the other hand, good contractors will make the architect's job much easier—calling to get design decisions worked out, anticipating needs, and finding solutions before they become problems. The low-quality contractor will put lights off center, put doors in the wrong place, paint over dust, forget outlets. The inept contractor will make the architect's life miserable and, by association, sully the architect's reputation in the eyes of the client.

7

Solutions to Power Problems

F irst, hire a reputable contractor with solid references and a clean background at the Better Business Bureau. Second, understand every clause of the contract; either learn it yourself or have your architect or lawyer lead you through. I'll talk about the standard AIA contract I recommend in "Management Solutions" in this section. Third, establish everyone's responsibilities.

At the beginning of negotiations, the owner needs to put everyone at ease. The owner needs to make clear how important everyone is to the project. I remember fondly those owners who've said at the beginning of the negotiation something like this:

"John, we're so glad we have you here today and we're confident we're going to be able to come to an acceptable contract for all of us. We have some concerns, I'm sure you have some concerns. We'd like to work through those today with the architect here and resolve the contract. We do have an alternate contractor if we can't come to terms, but we would much rather go with you, and I suppose you have some other jobs you could accept rather than go with us, but we hope we're your first choice as well. So, let's begin. About the payment schedule, what do you mean by . . ."

Why do I like this opening? Because it makes a lot of good negotiating moves all at once. First off, it has made the negotiation professional rather than personal—in other words, a business problem that must be solved. It has established who is in control. Owners who are reluctant to take charge of their project, either because they feel unqualified or fear offending the contractor or architect, will leave the project with a power vacuum at the top. Let everyone know that as owner, you are in charge of hiring the architect and contractor, aiming the design, setting the budget, communicating your needs, making the payments. You also need to let the architect know that she is in charge of design and that the contractor is in charge of execution.

Up until now you and the architect have been members of a team, but once you hire the contractor, you must accept him on that team. Traditionally, architects work to keep an exclusive relationship with the client, which puts the contractor in an adversarial role. This is counterproductive and has been rapidly changing in the world of high-end commercial construction. Viewing the participants as partners makes for a better, less contentious, more efficient relationship.

Now would be a good time to read the Negotiation section in the appendix.

8

Management Problems

Why don't contractors like to put together contracts that are an accurate representation of the work and prices? For the same reason chefs hate doing dishes. It's tedious work that you can't charge directly for. Drawing up contracts is something that the contractor and architect are expected to do gratis, as part of their job. Yet, when lawyers make contracts, they are well compensated.

It takes four to eight hours to write a good contract that includes the pay schedule, the time schedule, the bid breakdown, and the contract itself. At the last moments of contract negotiation, usually while the contractor's previous job is finishing up, there is often little time for this kind of involved work. The contractor hasn't received any money to put the contract together, nor does he have a guarantee that he's getting the job. Because of this, the contract is often cobbled together without all the safeguards that ensure the job goes well.

The architect often stays away from contract discussions to limit her own fiscal responsibility should anything go wrong. Suddenly it's up to an ill-prepared owner and a busy contractor to come to terms. As a result, many contracts aren't more than a few handwritten sheets on a "standard" bid form. Or the architect furnishes the standard AIA contract to the contractor, who inserts no modification and little specification.

9

Solutions to Management Problems

As we've said, the problem with the contracting phase is that the contractor is busy finishing his other projects and the architect is afraid of increasing her liability if she gives advice concerning the contract. Now is the time for the owner to step to the plate and help everyone get what they want: a beautiful project, on time and on budget.

So our owner must now arrange all the meetings, the time, date, and place as well as the subjects to be discussed. Be clear and let everyone know who's in control of this phase.

Also look at a few other contracts. Ask to see the contractor's and architect's standard form. For the most part, I use the American Institute of Architects Form A107, Abbreviated Form of Agreement Between Owner and Contractor for Construction Projects of Limited Scope Where the Basis of Payment Is a Stipulated Sum. This is the contract endorsed by the Council of General Contractors as well as the American Institute of Architects.

In order to make it a better document, though, you must make sure that quality specifications are included (see chapters 9 and 10 in this section). Set a deadline using the suggestions from the Time chapters in this section and set up a payment schedule using the advice from the Money chapters. In the "Contracts" section in the appendices of this book, you'll find the exact wording I recommend you use in the contract.

In addition, the AIA contract stipulates using arbitration for any disputes. I recommend that you change the wording of the contract to include the use of mediation as a first course of action. I explain dispute resolution in depth in Part Four, "Ending Construction," but the quick reason is that arbitration brings the dispute before a professional neutral who, after hearing the facts in a mini-trial, makes a decision for you. This will indeed feel like a trial and both sides will feel like adversaries. In mediation, a professional mediator helps the disputants come to a fair decision themselves. Mediation is much faster and cost-effective, and it also allows the parties to be able to continue working together. It's difficult to replace your contractor during the course of the job, and mediators will find a way to preserve the relationship if one exists. Verbiage for a mediation provision is included in the appendices as well as the address for the American Institute of Architects so that you can order AIA contracts.

You must, must, *must* demand and get a time schedule for the job from your contractor. Go through it with him to make sure that it makes sense and that he's thought the job through. Ask for a materials list at the same time. As the owner, you are forcing the contractor to do his homework *before* he gets his down payment. Most contractors are too busy to write an accurate time schedule or a careful materials list, and without being forced to do it, they will neglect it. In the end, a good time schedule and materials list will help the project immensely.

The materials list will also justify the contractor's down payment request. Contractors who request large down payments often use the money they receive for obligations not related to your job. Once the contractor lists all the materials and labor, he'll see that a smaller down payment is reasonable.

Contractors also ask for large down payments when they don't trust the clients to make prompt payment. Money is the fuel for construction, so I recommend that you address this concern by setting up a system for prompt payment. You can propose that the contractor give you three days' notice before he files a pay request. Once the pay request is received the architect then has two days to review and either approve or disapprove it. If everyone is in agreement, the owner immediately wires the money into the contractor's account.

Turn to the Contracts section in the appendix for a detailed look at an actual contract.

10

Quality
Problems

Your preparations during the contracting stage will decide whether you finish with a quality project or not. Often owners don't specify quality during this stage, instead trusting that quality will be delivered by the professionals they choose.

The problem is that quality has so many levels, and unless you specify *exactly what you want,* you won't get it. Either you'll pay too much money to get something you don't want or you'll pay less but get something that is unacceptable, and often quite difficult to correct. Without written specifications, the job you thought you agreed to might turn into something less, because there's nothing in the contract to force the contractor to do a first-rate quality job.

The plan could call for a Sheetrock wall. Fine. The contractor installs thin Sheetrock without insulation and gives it a standard finish. You move in and then you call the contractor because you can hear everything that's on the other side of the wall, your son put his hand through it, and you can see where the individual sheets of rock come together.

For the contractor to fix your problems, he'll have to remove all the Sheetrock from the wall and change it to ⅝-inch Sheetrock instead of ½-inch. He'll have to install sound insulation, "tape" the joints again, and then skim the whole wall with compound.

To some clients, the quality of his work the first time around would have been completely acceptable. Imagine if these second clients were going out of town and they asked the local carpenter to put up a wall when they were away. This carpenter does the fully insulated/skimmed/⅝ Sheetrock job. These second owners are going to have a heart attack when they see a bill for $1,200 instead of the $500 they were expecting.

Contractors in search of a competitive edge will lower their prices by hiring unlicensed or inexperienced subcontractors to do the job. In theory, they make up for this inexperience by careful management. Contractors would like to hire the best people for the job, but the people they are bidding against are using the unlicensed people as well, so everyone's in the same lowball mess.

Not that there aren't many good unlicensed subcontractors around (often, hiring an unlicensed subcontractor will give you that company's experienced owner to do the work), but when problems occur, now or ten years from now, you want the work in your home to be professional. Look at the houses that survive tornadoes, earthquakes and canyon fires. Every one of them was built and designed by professionals working to strict standards. When your three-hundred-pound boss leans on your sink, you want that sink to be supported properly, and licensed professionals are going to make sure of that.

During this first phase of contracting, it's easy to lose sight of our imaginary new kitchen and become focused solely on price and terms. Don't believe that a good plan is the only insurance for getting the job we want. Good specifications are essential, but they're of no use if the contractor can't meet them. Again, find a contractor that's best for your job.

While some items, like doorknob parts, can be clearly specified in the contract, other specifications will rely on the style of work that the contractor typically does. An inexpensive-grade, commercial contractor has radically different methods of installing cabinets than someone who specializes in high-end custom interiors. The bargain contractor has neither the manpower, the tools, nor the experience to make a $30,000 kitchen look as beautiful as it could. It may be level and square but the little details will be clumsy and the whole job will lack the finesse that makes a beautiful, worthwhile job.

11

Solutions to
Quality Problems

I t is essential for owners to establish a budget, then work with an architect and a contractor to plan a feasible design. If the budget is small, then the owner must decide whether (a) to limit the amount of work using the best-quality materials and execution or (b) to contract a larger amount of work with an interesting design but fewer top-quality materials. You could choose either a single cherry bookcase with raised panel doors and hand-rubbed finish or a whole wall of bookcases with painted cows on the doors. Both plans will interest competent architects and contractors. But only if the budget is generous should the owners consider the whole wall of cherry cabinets.

The architect will concentrate on designing solutions to meet your aesthetics and suit your practical needs. They are not experts at execution and that is why it's essential to use a competent contractor as a consultant during the design phase. During the contracting stage the contractor should specify what he intends to do so that you can show his specifications to the other contractors who are bidding the project to make sure they are intending to do the same job. It's in the best interest of this first contractor to specify what he'll do because otherwise he might be underbid by contractors planning to do less. Setting out what he intends to do will force competing contractors to bid on the same work, reducing their ability to underbid.

Here are some sample specifications that should figure in the bidding process.

General Conditions and Protection

- Amount of protection and furniture moving to be done by contractor

- Amount of protection and furniture moving to be done by owner

- Responsibility for rubbish removal

- Level of cleanliness during job

- Level of cleanliness at the end of job

Walls

- Stud type

- Stud thickness

- Stud frequency

- Sheetrock thickness

- Sheetrock type (waterproof or regular)

- Method of Sheetrock to stud attachment (screwed or nailed)

- Allowable defects in finish (joints between Sheetrock visible, scratches and pits allowed)

- Whether complete wall surface is skimmed with joint compound (form of Spackle)

Paint

- Whether existing walls will be scraped

- Allowable defects in finish (patches visible, scratches and pits allowed, old awkward repairs left)

- Spot-prime or all walls primed

- Type of primer

- Type and brand of finish paint

- Number of coats

Wood Floors

- Species and grade of new floor to be put down

- Whether hardwood floor repairs will involve removing whole boards so the hole is irregular and therefore less noticeable, or whether the repair will cut straight across the boards noticeably

- Grade of sandpaper to be used (down to 80 grit, 100 grit, or 120)

- Stained or not

- Number of stain samples for free

- Type and brand of polyurethane (oil- or water-based)

- Sheen (flat, semi, or gloss)

- Number of coats

- Whether he'll "screen" (sand lightly) between coats

Woodwork

- Who designs

- Are shop drawings provided by contractor?

- Type of wood to be used

- Defects acceptable (gaps in molding, gap to wall, nail holes visible)

- Type of finish

Tile work

- Layout and design by?

- Type and color of tile

- Substrate type (mud, Wonderboard, water resistant Sheetrock, Sheetrock, existing conditions)

- Adhesive type

- Warrantee length against cracking

Electrical

- Whether existing code violations will be addressed

- Work to be done to panel

- Whether electrician has his own license or is working under someone else's

- Whether work will be inspected

Plumbing

- Current drain times for one gallon of water at each drain

- Current fill times for one gallon of water at each faucet

- Whether he'll be addressing existing code violations

- Type of supply material (copper or PVC)

- Type of sanitary piping material (cast iron, PVC)

- Size of all drain lines

- Use of antihammer columns at faucets

HVAC (Heating, Venting, Air-Conditioning)

- Temperature to which the space will be cooled to on a 105° day

- Temperature to which the space will be heated to on a −15° day

- Decibels the system will produce

- Number of diffusers

- Type of ductwork (flexible or rigid, insulated or not)

NOTE: All subcontractors must be licensed and insured, and copies of their licenses and insurance must be provided to the owner.

This final note levels the playing field so that all of the contractors will hire professional subs, and it will prevent a lowball bid with lowball subcontractors.

In all of these areas, there's a cheap way to do things and a more expensive way to do them. I have found that the more expensive way of doing things is almost always better. Ask your architect and contractor for their advice.

All of these specifications need to make it into your contract, either as part of the drawings (which is the basis of your contract) or as an attached sheet to the contract.

What happens if you don't have much money, say $3,000, you need the room added, and you get three bids, for $5,000, $5,000, and $2,885.

You should ask the two contractors who bid $5,000 to take out everything but the essentials, and you offer to throw them a party at the end. They come down to $4,800 and $4,825. Is it possible to get a good job out of the low bidder? Yes, but it's risky. To improve your chances, do the following:

1. Check his references carefully, and check with the Better Business Bureau and Consumer Affairs. (Do this on the most expensive bidder as well.) If they don't have good things to say, face the fact that you will have to wait until you have more money saved to add that room.

2. Tell the low contractor that he's more expensive than the rest (in other words, lie) and you want to see why. Get a complete list of specifications outlining exactly how he's doing the work and compare it to the detailed bid from your consultant contractor. (Don't succumb to the temptation to try to get him down to $2,500.)

3. Learn what this contractor needs in order to work efficiently and try to furnish it. See what you can do to help out the contractor. You should clear out the rooms and protect the furniture and floors yourself. Room protection is one category in which the lower-priced contractors skimp. Give this contractor plenty of room to work. Check in often to make sure that he's progressing. Make sure he keeps on your contracted schedule. There will be many more suggestions in the "Beginning Construction" and "Ending Construction" sections. Pay close attention to them.

4. Treat the contractor's office (which may well be his wife) very well. When things go wrong, and they're more likely to with the bargain contractor, you'll want someone on your side to advocate that the contractor takes care of the problem responsibly. As with many things in life, the best time to make friends is before there's a problem.

The Finleys—
Contracting in
Everyone's Best
Interest

Michelle and Tom Finley were sitting at their kitchen table, looking at the three sets of bids. It was dark outside and they could see their reflection in the kitchen window, the storm window blurring their silhouettes. They had two estimates other than DeTomaso's. DeTomaso's was the longest and most detailed. Chris had gone to make a call and the Finleys were waiting for her return.

Chris came back into the room. "We could first try to talk DeTomaso down."

"I don't understand why DeTomaso's bid is twenty-eight thousand when he knew that our overall budget was twenty-five thousand. Three thousand for architecture and permits. Twenty-two thousand for him."

Michelle's voice was reasonable. "He said that was the least he could charge for all the work we wanted done."

"This other bid here is fifteen."

Chris spoke quickly. "That's without the cabinets and appliances."

Tom continued, "And when you include the appliances and cabinets, they're twenty-one-fifty. Within the budget. I'm not spending more than our budget, DeTomaso or not. We can pay him his two hundred fifty dollars and wish him a nice day."

Chris piped in: "DeTomaso says he wants to supply the cabinets and appliances so that his warrantee covers those as well. If there's any problem with anything, it's all his responsibility. I can't tell you how often I've seen missing parts on faucets and appliances and damaged cabinets, and then the client is trying to return them."

"But he wants to add twenty percent for that," Tom said. "One-fifth of their value so that if they have a damaged door, he'll get a new one. I could order them over the phone."

There was a silence, their lighted faces looming in the kitchen window.

Suddenly, their faces glowed brighter and then subsided as truck headlights swung past them and turned into the driveway. The sharp knock at the kitchen door brought DeTomaso into the room.

"I see your faces. I know you're talking about me. What have we decided?"

Michelle looked down at the other bids. "Everyone's within our budget except you. We told you the budget and you're over it."

"So you tell me, if you said you want the Sistine Chapel for a hundred thousand dollars, would you fault me for going over your budget? I can't do your job for twenty-two thousand dollars. I do a bad job for that and then you hate me and Ms. Layner hates me and you tell all your friends. If you can't afford me and hire my competition, at least afterward you tell everyone, 'Ah, I should have hired DeTomaso. I see why he was worth more money.' "

As much as Tom hated DeTomaso's price he really liked the guy. "So in our shoes, what would you do, Mr. DeTomaso?"

"I would ask the good Mr. DeTomaso for his recommendations on how to get rid of six thousand dollars out of this project."

"Question asked."

"You can't. The design is superb, the execution is superb. Pay the extra six thousand dollars."

Tom's face flushed with frustration. "That is very funny, Mr. DeTomaso, but I will not pay over our budget."

No one said anything.

Chris finally broke the silence. "Mr. DeTomaso, your price was a surprise to us because we had asked all along that you help us stay within the budget. I thought what I was designing was within that. We all would like to work with you and I would certainly like to work with you in the future. Can you help us to understand why we're overbudget and how we can find a way to work together?"

DeTomaso shrugged his shoulders. "I make a mistake. I don't include the floor in my original figuring and I underestimated what my electrician and plumber would come in at. I thought we were going to be fine but we are not. This is my price."

It was Thursday afternoon and Michelle had just come back to the house for lunch. She taught at a local junior college close enough to home that she didn't have to be around her students during the lunch break. The phone rang and Michelle picked it up. Most of Michelle and Tom's friends knew they both worked and didn't call during the day—except with bad news that they wanted to tell the machine.

"Hello, Mrs. Finley, this is Giovanni DeTomaso."

"Oh, yes, how are you?"

"I feel very bad about my price."

"Yes, so do we." Michelle felt like accommodating him in some way, but she fought these instincts. She knew Tom was standing fast on twenty-five thousand for everything included, and she knew he was right. If they had to hire Dynamic Construction they would.

"I would like to just lower my price six thousand dollars, but I know that then it doesn't work out for any of us."

"Yes, I understand this. It's just that we've worked so hard on our plan and we truly like it and Dynamic and Mark Thrasher both have prices that are within our budget."

"I understood this from last night and I think to myself how I can be six thousand dollars more than them. Perhaps two thousand, but six?"

"Well, they don't have the appliances and the cabinets in their number—"

"Then my price is twenty! Of course they are cheaper."

"No, Mr. DeTomaso, we've added in the price of the cabinets, it's just that we save twenty percent. That's fourteen hundred dollars right there."

"This is fourteen hundred dollars to get my complete warrantee on the cabinets and the appliances. I order them, I specify them, I take responsibility if they come in incorrect."

"Yes, we understand that. I'm just trying to explain why you are too much for us to afford."

"Listen, you are foolish not to afford me."

"Then, Mr. DeTomaso, bring your price down, because we are not paying more than twenty-two thousand to have this work done."

There was silence on the other end of the phone. Michelle could picture DeTomaso's face as he attempted not to scream at her.

When he spoke, she appreciated his control. "It is my feeling that you think you are getting the same work for twenty-two thousand from these other companies, but I know they are not giving you what I am giving you. Until you know this, you have no choice but to dismiss me. May I see the other bids?"

"I'm not sure if that's ethical."

"Then let me write down everything that I intend to do, with my specifications, and you give this to these other contractors and you tell me then what their price is."

"That sounds like a lot of work."

"One, you've paid me two hundred fifty dollars so far. I'm not in the hole on this. Two, I like you and I don't want to see you get taken for a ride. Three, I don't like it when people underbid work. Four, I want to do your job."

"Very well, but I would need this right away. Our schedule says we hire our contractor within the week."

"I have this for you in two days."

Tom was standing in the kitchen with Mark Thrasher, the contractor who came in at $21,500. Thrasher was a young man with hair that stood straight up in a pantomime of his energy. He was perplexed at DeTomaso's list. "I think a lot of this is overkill."

"Like what?" Tom said.

"Well, I was going to tile over the existing floor in the kitchen."

"With ceramic twelve-by-twelves? Won't they crack?"

"It's ceramic?" Thrasher's face flushed as he flipped open the plans looking for the spec. "It says here in floor finishes: twelve-by-twelve tile style to be decided. It doesn't say ceramic; I figured it for vinyl twelve-by-twelve."

Tom's face flushed now as he wrote this down on the list. He was working to control his temper. When he and Michelle had discussed meeting with Thrasher, Michelle was concerned Tom might get angry if things didn't go right. She didn't want to come home to find any columns cut in half. "What else is overkill?"

"Backing up, should I price the kitchen floor for ceramic?"

Tom shook his head. "I don't know. It costs that much money?"

"That's why I guess I was figuring vinyl from the start. This is a bouncy floor. I'd have to reinforce the floor maybe from below, then maybe put down a layer of plywood, then cut the tile. With the center island, and on a diamond pattern, it's another two thousand dollars. Besides, ceramic floors are kind of rough on the glassware and the knees."

"Well, leave it out of the bid for now. What else is overkill?"

"Well, he's got a whole new electric panel. You don't need that. We'll just add to what's there."

"DeTomaso says there's not enough room."

Thrasher's face went red again. "Did I see the panel? I don't think I saw it last time."

Tom brought him out into the utility room, moved aside a painting, and opened up the cover on the box.

Sweat popped up on Thrasher's forehead like dew on a cold soda can. "This is an old-style box." Thrasher gave a big sigh. "Yes, you want to add the electric oven, the clothes dryer, you're going to have to change the panel. That's a lot of money. Why don't you keep the gas range?"

"My wife wants the electric oven for baking."

"It's seven hundred bucks. Maybe eight. Use gas, it's already there and just pipe off to the side for the dryer. You're going to vent it outside anyway."

Tom wrote it down. "What do you think about buying the cabinets and the appliances?"

"I don't do that. Too many times, things go wrong. Have the guys selling you the cabinets come in here and draw it out and get them to agree to warrantee the appliances or something."

"They don't want to come in here and do that either. They say that they can't be responsible for what the contractor does."

"I just don't want to be mixed up in that. I've been burned too many times."

Tom looked at Thrasher, trying to see inside him. Why had he been burned too many times? he thought to himself.

Thrasher caught the look. "Listen, I'd like to do the job, and if ordering the cabinets is what would make the deal for you, I'll do it."

"Thanks, we'll be getting back to you, and I really appreciate the time you've put in. Is there anything else in these specs that you're not planning on doing?"

"Well, his painting method is over the top. We're just planning on standard work here and I'm half the cost; I imagine he's probably going to be doing a better job since he's planning on laminating all the walls straight."

"What does that mean?"

"He's planning on putting Sheetrock over all your existing walls to make them straight. We're going to just plaster and patch them."

"What's on the plans?"

Mark opened up the plans. "Yeah, it says here laminate, but I knew what your price wanted to be."

Tom nodded. "You're thinking the right way. I wish you'd pointed that out in your bid. Anything else?"

"Do you know what he's talking about when he says he's biscuiting the miters in the door casings?"

Tom and Michelle Finley were getting ready for bed, each walking back and forth into the bathroom. Spring was coming and the windows were open, the light curtains fluttering out against the screens.

"So what do we do?" Tom asked.

"It sounds like the other prices were less because they were doing things more simply. When you add those things up, it's a lot of money. I say we go back to DeTomaso, ask him if he can do a vinyl tile floor, a gas oven and dryer instead of the electric, keep the old panel, and see if he would agree to meet with the kitchen cabinet people when they come but we'd buy the cabinets ourselves. See if he can do it for fifteen thousand. Plus the eight for the cabinets and we're at twenty-three. A thousand more than we wanted."

"DeTomaso says he'd like to change the panel anyway but he understands our point. He agrees that a vinyl floor is better. He says it's one of his rules to supply everything, including cabinets, but he can save us some money while making some himself if he makes the counters. His price now is twenty-five thousand if we let him use the house to show other people through."

"Now what? You raised our ceiling to twenty-three thousand. Do we go higher? Remember, we still have three thousand to Chris and there could easily be another three thousand in extras."

"Well, we get a hundred and fifty back from our bid if we hire DeTomaso, right?"

"Yes."

"And listen, it would have taken time if we had bought the cabinets ourselves and something would probably screw up."

"Do we want the walls laminated?"

"What does Chris think?"

"She says it would look a lot crisper."

"Do we like crisper? The rest of the house is kind of bumpy and I like it. It looks like plaster."

"It *is* plaster."

"But then the cabinets don't go up as straight."

"Call DeTomaso."

"DeTomaso says we're insane but he likes us. He says he can skim the walls close to flat around the cabinets with a little more effort, so the price is twenty-four thousand twenty-five dollars, but he'll do it for twenty-three thousand nine hundred and ninety-nine as long as we tell everyone he's the best contractor in the world."

"Sold."

Chris, DeTomaso, and the Finleys were gathered around the kitchen table, three copies of DeTomaso's contract laid out. "You see I use the standard AIA contract. I fill in all the slots, and what I don't fill in, I put the X's. I even put in the completion date."

Tom spoke up. "How about here where it says liquidated damages per day if you are late? There's an X there. Did we agree that there wouldn't be a penalty?"

DeTomaso looked uncomfortable. "You give me a bonus if I'm early?"

Tom looked at Michelle and got her silent nod. "Yes, I think that's fair. We'd love you to be early and we certainly don't want you to be late. I think if we have this date here without a penalty or bonus, then it's worthless. I don't want to have you late and then my only recourse is to be grumpy."

"How much is this bonus?"

Michelle spoke now. "I'm not sure what's standard. We were thinking of putting a week's grace on either side of the due date; then twenty-five dollars a day for you if you're early, twenty-five dollars a day for us if you're late."

DeTomaso thought about that. "I never agree to penalty clauses but this doesn't seem unfair. Before I agree to that, let me bring up one change I like to make to this contract. They say if we have a dispute, God forbid, we go to arbitration. I don't like arbitration because there's lawyers, there's me against you, somebody who hears us talk for two hours makes a decision. I like mediation where somebody gets between us and sorts things out but it's still us that decide what we do. Only, it has to be good enough for each of us or we go on to arbitration. There's a guy who does it by phone so you can resolve a dispute same day it happens almost. It's a hundred dollars a half hour, we split. How about that?"

Michelle looked at Chris. "Have you ever heard of this?"

"Giovanni gave me the brochure. It actually sounds very good. Otherwise, if we have a dispute, we have to go to arbitration. If we choose not to do that, I'll have to play mediator, and I haven't been trained to be a mediator."

"Do you think we need this, Giovanni?" Tom asked.

"I hope with all my prayers we don't, just like I hope I don't pay you twenty-five dollars."

Tom looked at Michelle and together they said, "Fine."

Contracting Checklist

Money

- Use the consultant contractor's bid to compare second and third bids.

- Use the consultant contractor to make sure that the other contractors don't underbid the job.

- Add nonmonetary benefits (e.g., free publicity, professional cleaning) to make the deal better for both sides.

Time

- Enforce deadlines during this phase to show their importance to you.

- Set a time line for the bidding process and keep to it.

- Make sure all permits, etc., are in place or in the works.

- Avoid wasting time during the contracting stage that you'll need during the construction phase.

Power

- Keep contractor, owner, and architect thinking of the shared goal, a beautiful project on time and on budget.

- Acknowledge the contributions of each party at the onset of negotiations.

- Make the payment schedule fair and a motivator in the project.

Management

- The owner controls the contracting stage.

- Choose the correct contract.

- Demand a written time schedule.

- Decide on a dispute management system.

Quality

- Specify exact quality level in contract for carpentry joints, tiling joints, Sheetrock finish, plastering, and paint.

- Pay a premium for first-quality workmanship.

Part Three

Beginning Construction

1

The Hamptons— Deep Sleep in the Nightmare Kitchen

L arry was adjusting his tie as he came downstairs, too eager to finish in front of the mirror in their bedroom. "Frank here yet?"

"Not ye-et," Cindy said in a singsong. Larry had been asking since he got up, like a kid at Christmas. Now Cindy glanced outside. It was a dark morning, the clouds covering what little morning sun there was. The sky felt low and comforting. Not raining yet but Cindy knew there would be rain on her windshield on her way to work.

"He's still coming, though?" Larry said.

Cindy knew Frank would come. It felt like they had made a little pact with the devil and the devil always showed. Suddenly, lights swiveled through the kitchen and Cindy looked out. They were "fog" lights Frank must have installed during a flush period. For a moment, the brightness of the lights concealed the bailing wire that held the rest of the Volvo together. The car hadn't been washed in some time and Cindy guessed no car wash manager would let him in, fearful the spinning brushes would get caught in the homemade hardware Frank had tied the car together with over the years. The whole Volvo had attained a kind of organic form, readying itself to crumble into the earth. The headlights dimmed brown and vanished from the kitchen ceiling.

Larry was now standing beside Cindy. Both had tight smiles as they tried to imagine that this ramshackle car and their beautiful kitchen would have Frank in common.

The doors opened after some goodwilled pushing (Frank was aware they were watching) and two more people piled out of the backseat. They popped up the rear hatch, and suddenly everyone was pulling things out of the back of the car and placing them on the driveway.

Before the Hamptons knew it, they'd lost the opportunity to tell Frank they had second thoughts.

Frank was all smiles as he bounded up the stairs. "Good morning." Frank put his hand on his hip where his beeper suddenly chirped. "Do you mind if I use your phone?"

Cindy half nodded at Frank as he walked by her into the kitchen. He picked up the phone and pounded out the number.

Larry tried to pull Cindy out of the room but she was listening. The other party answered and Frank said, "This is Frank, who's this?"

Frank listened for a moment. Suddenly he said again, "Hello? Hello?" then looked at the phone in a pantomime of wonder. As he hung up, the sound of the tinny imprisoned voice came out of the earpiece, "Frank, you bastard, you owe me money!"

Frank, Larry, and Cindy then decided together, without speaking a word, that Frank had received a page from an out-of-service number. Somehow, believing anything else was too difficult.

Cindy brightened. "Did you bring a contract for us?"

"Yeah, I was just finishing that. Let me get it out of the car."

They watched Frank go out to the car and paw about at the papers that lay on the dashboard, wrinkled from windshield condensation.

Larry couldn't watch anymore. He couldn't speak either. He walked upstairs to get his briefcase. He came back down after a minute. Cindy hadn't torn herself away from the window.

Larry said, "Well, at least now we know why he was so cheap."

"Do you think this will be okay?"

"Well, it looks like he has the tools. He'll be fine. We're not hiring him to be our lawyer; and if he was any more organized, I doubt he'd be in this business."

Frank threw open the door, startling Larry and Cindy.

"You know, this is ridiculous," Frank said, holding up the half-blank contract. "Basically, I'm putting in the kitchen, taking down this wall. You know it, I know it. What else is there?"

"Well, painting, flooring—"

Frank took her words like dictation, a smell of nervousness coming off him. "Maybe it would be better if I just took this home tonight, typed it up, and brought it in tomorrow. The guys are really raring to go and I hate to pay them to just stand around."

"If you want to wait for your check until tomorrow."

Frank looked at her. "Then you can have a handwritten contract, but I'm not starting without a check. Do you honestly think I'm going to do the work any differently because of a contract? I'm more interested in getting the other two-thirds of the money and keeping you as a steady customer. Personally, I apologize; this isn't a proper contract. But I'll tell you what: Let me give you this handwritten contract. Give me the check. Tomorrow I'll give you a proper contract."

Cindy scowled at the bill of sale form Frank had. "I don't know. Larry?"

"I've got to get to work." He had his briefcase and was standing at the door. "Frank, just give us the proper contract tomorrow. Cindy, if we're going to do this, we might as well jump in. Go ahead, give him the check and let's get on with this."

"Great," Frank said. He turned back to his men while Cindy got out the checkbook. "Go ahead and set up the tools by the kitchen table."

As Cindy wrote out the check she pointed with her head toward the living room. "You'll make sure everything is out of harm's way."

"Of course. I may not be the best at contracts, but wait until you see what we can do with a box of screws and some joint compound."

Frank was smiling. Cindy felt like she was falling off a cliff.

As soon as the Hamptons left for work, their telephone numbers carefully noted down on the refrigerator, Frank checked the bank location on the check, drove there, and cashed it. It was as good as a certified check but not nearly as hard to get. People always figured they have at least until that night to stop the check. Frank knew from experience. Not that he didn't start the guys before he left. Not that he wasn't going back to the Hamptons' as soon as he could. It was just important to get the money in his hands.

Larry liked driving in the Pathfinder alone. He could play the stereo loud. He could keep his coat on and the heat off. It had been a good day and he was excited to get home. He imagined what he would see there. He had waited until noon to call, to let Frank get himself settled in. He was actually surprised to learn that everything was going great. They had already got the wall between the kitchen and the den halfway down when he'd called. Perhaps he had guessed right about Frank. That he was the kind of guy who could get things done. So paperwork wasn't his strong point. He had been in the phone book and things seemed to be turning out okay. Cindy could settle down now, too. He had called after he talked to Frank to let her know the good news. They almost got together for lunch to celebrate.

Larry pulled into the driveway. All the lights were on inside the house. His son's bedroom light was on, too. He felt invincible as he sprang up the steps. That was the thing. People were always willing to spend money for nothing. Not willing to take a bit of a risk sometimes. Tomorrow they'd have the real contract. On schedule.

As he walked into the house, the air swirled tangibly around the edge of the door. Why could he suddenly see the air? Larry thought to himself. As his eyes adjusted, he could see that the air was fairly sparkling—tiny bits of light, glinting all around him. His eyes focused on Cindy's mother's china cabinet. It was covered in a layer of plaster dust. The entire house was covered with a thin layer. He could see it clearly on their upholstery except the dark spots where his son sat after he came home from school. In the back of the house he could hear his son coughing. Suddenly Larry panicked. He had completely forgotten about his son's asthma.

Cindy was standing in the middle of what had been their kitchen. Her eyes were rimmed with red and she had white circles around her nostrils where she had been breathing in this plaster. She was seething in rage, immobilized by venom. Around her lay haphazard piles of plaster and dirty two-by-fours. Larry's nostrils stung from the sharp smell of mold and rusting steel lath. It looked as if there had been an earthquake and the kitchen had been demolished. Then, apparently, a rescue team had come, scattered their power tools and oil-stained lunch bags around the kitchen, knocked over a ladder, and left a web of power cords plugged in and tangled across ruin. All of the workers' possessions were under this rubble. Didn't these people have homes?

"Larry, Howard is coughing. I tried calling Frank. My crystal is ruined. He didn't even put away the radio. All the food is covered in this filth. Call him, Larry."

The phone rang at that moment and Cindy picked it up, staring at Larry. "Yes? . . . Frank! We are very displeased, very. You've left our home a shamb—what?" Cindy listened, then started again. "I don't care . . ." There was again a long pause, her face growing pale. "You're insured, though, Frank?" Another pause. "Well, you'll be back tomorrow . . . Okay, yes, we'll see you then." Cindy hung up the phone and looked at Larry. Her face was palest white.

"One of his guys fell off a ladder, he's got a compound fracture. They had to take him to the hospital." Cindy looked distractedly out the window, shocked at how subdued she'd become. It worried her in a way she couldn't put a finger on. "He apologized for leaving the house in such a mess. They were just ready to clean up."

"Cindy, if they don't have insurance—"

"No, he said he does." Cindy was barely breathing. She had let their homeowner's insurance lapse. "He felt bad. He'll be in tomorrow. He offered to come tonight."

"How about the crystal, Cindy? He would have cleaned that? Cindy, this guy is an ass."

"Larry, you are the one who didn't want to spend the money. Should we fire him and hire someone else?" Cindy's voice was trembling. "Do you want to get sued by him and this guy who fell off the ladder?"

"How are those related?"

She was nearly screaming now. "As long as Frank is here, the guy who fell off the ladder will be working, and everything will be fine. Just give him until tomorrow, and then we'll see."

"Why are you defending him, Cindy?"

"I'm not. I just don't want things to go wrong. If we fire Frank, the guy gets laid off. Then he could sue us. It scares me."

The rain of the previous day was gone and the morning air felt bright. Upstairs in the bedrooms the house felt clean enough. Howard, their son, had been coughing and wheezing through the night, so Cindy suggested that they go out for breakfast. The alternative was a dusty box of Cheerios.

Larry and Cindy talked on the phone during the day but were afraid to call the house to see if Frank was there. Silently, they were hoping somehow a miracle would take place, that when they came home, they would find their house just as they had hoped. The kitchen removed, everything clean and neat. Maybe even some of the new cabinets installed. They didn't realize it, but they talked about everything except the house, seizing on topic after topic, their voices carrying the constant message, "Will everything be all right? Will everything be all right? Will everything be all right?"

It was four-thirty when Larry called Cindy to tell her that he would pick her up after work. While they were talking, unbeknownst to them the front screen door of their house hissed shut, partially obscuring the official notice taped eye-high on their door.

The Pathfinder wound its way through suburban streets, Larry and Cindy looking ahead for their house. "It's a little ridiculous," Cindy said. "We're driving along like we're on our way to a funeral home. I'm sure Frank took care of things." She didn't look at Larry as she said it.

As they pulled up they could make out the huge pile of rubbish stacked neatly at the curb. Larry hopped out of the car and Cindy followed through the back door in a hurry to see what had been done.

The kitchen had been cleaned. Electrical wires still hung down from the ceiling like the guts of some dead house, but the plaster had been knocked back, the appliances removed. There were still a few wood studs left where the center wall had been, but basically the kitchen looked okay.

"Larry!" Cindy screamed in pleasure. "He even cleaned the crystal. Look."

In fact, the crystal had been washed and the china cabinet had been covered with a plastic drop cloth.

"Not bad. I guess if the guy hadn't fallen off the ladder, this is what he would have done yesterday. I guess you were right. I can't believe this."

Both of them were smiling, suddenly transformed.

"Oooh, Larry," Cindy said, "could you go out and get my purse, I left it in the car."

Larry got the purse, but as he started back, he saw he had left white plaster-dust footprints leading out to the truck. He stared at the outlines of his feet for a minute, then danced a little hustle. Finishing, he looked back at the scatter of his footprints. Just like the dance lessons he took in the seventies.

He started back up the driveway toward the kitchen and then

realized they'd have to use the front door for a while or the house would be full of white footprints.

Changing course, he went up the steps, pulled out his keys, and opened the screen door. There was a note taped to the door. Larry pulled it off as he unlocked the door. The letter was from the village and Larry wondered if he had unpaid parking tickets on the Pathfinder.

"Why'd you come in that way?" Cindy asked.

"Look at your shoes. I didn't want to track dust around. Have you got any unpaid tickets on your car?"

Cindy screwed up her face. "No, why?"

"We got something from the village." Larry put down the purse and ripped open the envelope knowing full well that it contained some sort of bad news. Cindy moved alongside Larry to see what it said.

NOTICE TO CEASE AND DESIST CONSTRUCTION

You are hereby notified and commanded to cease all construction work currently engaged in. You are in violation of the law. The city of Bridgecamen must be notified of any work before it is begun. Proper plans must be submitted and approvals received before any work may commence. Violation of this notice carries a maximum penalty of $10,000.

They read the notice together, then Larry folded it up quietly and returned it to the envelope. Cindy's voice was soft. "Did we know we were supposed to get a building permit?"

Larry shook his head. "No."

Cindy was in a daze. "Is this why Frank was so cheap? Is this his fault? Shouldn't he have taken out the permit?"

"You would think," Larry said, springing to life. "It probably costs thirty-five bucks to get a permit and he didn't want to spend the money."

"I can't believe this. He wanted to save thirty-five dollars and so now they're threatening us with a ten-thousand-dollar fine," Cindy said. "Call him, Larry. This isn't fair."

In the morning Larry and Cindy were surprised to find Frank sitting on their doorstep. He turned around and stood up as soon as he heard Cindy opening their door. She kept the screen door closed.

"Good morning, Mrs. Hampton. I know I'm probably the last person you want to see right now but I'd like you to hear me out. I admit I left your place a mess on the first night but that was because Louis fell off the ladder and we had to leave in a hurry. Yesterday we worked very hard to straighten everything out—everything you were concerned with and everything I was concerned with. Getting a letter from the building department is bad, but that's your architect's fault. She should have filed the job and I'm pretty sure I told her that or at least asked her if she was going to file the job. I've done a lot of jobs without filing and I'm very sorry we got caught on this one but we did.

"Now, for me, if you fire me, I'm in big trouble. I've had a rough year and if I lose this job I'm afraid my wife's going to leave me and take the kids because we just don't have any money and we've been having problems because of it. I know that's not your fault, it's mine. I'm just trying to do a real good job for you and I'm sure we can get this permit thing worked out. I'm sure the notice is scary but we can work it out."

Cindy hadn't said anything and Larry had come in behind her and heard most of what Frank had to say. The screen door was still closed between them and both Cindy's and Larry's eyes were circled from the night before. Cindy spoke first. "I think it's very unfair to tell us your personal problems, Frank. You should have got us the building permit. What's going to happen now?"

Frank could see the opening and he flew delicately into it. "As I recall, your designer wasn't licensed and that's why she couldn't pull the permit. I know a real good engineer, an old friend of mine, who could do the job for you. He knows people down at the building department and I think he could get the job done for us."

Cindy turned to Larry. "What do you think?"

Larry was bone-tired. Maybe Frank was right, he thought. Perhaps last night's note scared them more than it should have.

"Frank, I'll tell you what," Larry said. "You line us up an engineer to get the permit. If that works out and the fault isn't yours, we'll hire you back. Give me a call at my office and tell me when we can meet this man."

Frank nodded solemnly. "Thank you, Mr. and Mrs. Hampton. I'll get right to it. I'm very sorry about all this and I'll try to set things right."

The kitchen had not changed in the last week; the plastic sheeting that had pleased Cindy so much on the china cabinet was still there. The raw plaster edges of the former walls were still gaping open, electrical wires hanging lewdly through the space. Standing in the center of the room was Frank, who hadn't been back until now. Beside him was the engineer, a short, Indian man in a gray suit and tie. Standing beside him was Larry, then Cindy. All of them were staring into the exposed rafters of the ceiling and the two-by-fours bracing them from the floor.

The engineer spoke in his ringing accent: "I'm surprised there seems to be no deflection in the ceiling yet. This is the load-bearing wall. To remove it will bring the house down on itself. You did not think of this?"

Frank said quickly, "I was just following the architect's plan. That was her job."

Mr. Nostrami fought for control of his voice. "If there was an architect, then this architect must be called in now. This is inexcusable. There must be an engineer consulted before removing walls— this is thoughtless. Who is the architect? Where are these plans?"

"The plans are right here," Larry said, embarrassed that he was somehow being found wanting—a bad manager.

The engineer looked straight to the lower edge of the plans. "These plans are not stamped. There was no engineer. Were you arranging to get these stamped?" A ball of tension built up in Mr.

Nostrami as his frustration at shoddy work outpaced his ability to express it. He stopped speaking and looked at the drawings. Everyone else was quiet.

He began again more calmly. "Were you trying to have your plans stamped by an engineer as a favor?"

Cindy looked embarrassed for a moment and then spoke honestly. "Well, yes. Frank said he knew—"

The violence of Mr. Nostrami's voice shook everyone. "Do you people think that engineers are so thirsty for your money or the affection of a contractor that they will blindly stamp a set of drawings which instruct the builder to cause the collapse of your second floor? Frank asked me in to take a look at your situation and my loyalty to him ends now in my recommendation. You must hire a qualified professional engineer. He or she will submit a proper set of drawings to the chief plan examiner of Bridgecamen, who will review the safety of the plans. Upon his approval, Frank will be able to pull your building permit. Then you can finish this kitchen and resume your life."

"Thank you," Cindy said, looking as helpless and childlike as Larry had ever seen her. "Could you do this for us?"

Mr. Nostrami turned to Larry, who nodded mutely in agreement.

With a look of disgust, Mr. Nostrami said, "Very well. I'll start on this tomorrow."

"Nostrami-Pierce, Nostrami speaking."

"Hello, Mr. Nostrami, Larry Hampton. I was wondering whether you were close with our new plans."

"Good that you've called, Mr. Hampton. I've been waiting for my contract back from you."

"What contract?"

"I sent a contract—let me see—yes, two weeks ago. You were to sign and return it with a down payment so I could begin work on your plans. You did not receive it?"

Larry waited until after he'd hung up the phone to start screaming at Mr. Nostrami.

. . .

Frank knocked on the door and waited for Mrs. Hampton to open it. She had called the night before and asked him to come over. Frank was doubly nervous. He was afraid she had called him over either to serve him with a lawsuit or to ask him to start immediately. In a queer twist, the immediate start would be worse. He had no money. All of their down payment was gone. It had been six weeks since they'd given him the check and he hadn't had any other jobs going in the meantime. This was all he'd had lined up. But there were personal bills, business bills, some new pants, and the drill he'd bought on credit just for the job.

Cindy opened the door, looking calm in a beige suit she'd probably worn to work.

"Thanks for coming, Frank. We got the new plans from Mr. Nostrami last night and we couldn't understand them and we thought you could."

Frank felt a surge of pride as he reached for the plans. These plans were stamped and they showed in their hazy blueprint that there was to be a twelve-inch steel beam bisecting the kitchen.

"Very good."

"What is?" Cindy asked.

"Mr. Nostrami put in a steel beam to reinforce your opening and keep your second floor in the air. Very good."

"How will it look?"

"At this point you don't have much choice. Besides, you'll hardly notice it. Mrs. Hampton, sit back now, we've got our plan and soon our approval. I'll get this beam fabricated and we'll get rolling."

"Will we see you tomorrow, Frank?"

Frank's face flushed now as he could feel his heart begin to race. "As you know, Mrs. Hampton, stopping the job like this has really screwed me up. I had declined work so I could do your project, and when your project stopped, I didn't have anything else lined up."

Frank could feel Mrs. Hampton's eyes on him and he had to look down. "I hate to say this but I'm out of money."

"But you haven't done anything, Frank. You worked for two days. You haven't hired any men, you could have got another job."

"But I was waiting for you to—"

"I don't know about construction, you do. If we needed a permit, you should have known about it, just like you should have known that this wall was holding up the ceiling. Instead, you knock it down. All you had to do was look in the basement. Was that too much for you? This is ridiculous. And now you have the audacity to ask me for money while we're the people who are sitting in this dust and mess. You're asking me for money because you were out of work? Who put you out of work? Me? No, Frank, you put yourself out of work. I expect to see you here tomorrow and I expect you to get under way."

Frank looked at her and stuttered, "I-I . . ." Overcome, he backed out of the house, unable to answer her.

To Cindy's great amazement, Frank showed up the next morning. He stepped out at midmorning, but when he came back, he was in a very good mood.

The kitchen slowly began to come together. Frank brought in a man named Bruce, who Frank announced was the best carpenter he knew. Bruce was a tall, lanky man who spoke of his many accomplishments. He started out great, but increasingly he seemed to Cindy to be a drinker. He loved to talk when she stopped by, coming in close to her as he explained what he was doing to the walls. What he was doing to the walls seemed to involve nailing pieces of wood together in a somewhat crooked fashion and then asking for her approval when she walked by. She had no idea what she was looking at, so she always said "Fine" just to get away from him and back into her bedroom.

2

Money
Problems

Beginning construction is like a first date, filled with anxiety and improbable expectations. Because of its novelty,
the signs of trouble during the beginning of construction
are often overlooked or rationalized, just as a hapless teenage girl
may overlook her date's sudden realization that his car has run out of
gas.

It is important for the owners to trust their instincts. Often, when
I have made a mistake in hiring a subcontractor, I can look back and
see that they warned me in some subtle way of their true nature. But
when I saw these signs, I ignored them for fear of being overly cau-
tious (and of losing a good deal).

I once went to inspect a cabinetmaker's shop and saw many nice-
looking cabinets standing out on the floor, a large crew working away,
and a lot of sawdust. It surprised me, though, that this crew was
working on small table saws with hand clamps while around them

stood massive industrial machines, unused. This cabinetmaker's prices were very good, and even though I wondered why he wasn't using the industrial machines, I never asked. Obviously, he knew what he was doing.

I ordered one hundred pieces of four-by-four panels from him, and when they were delivered a month later—just in the nick of time—I noted that they weren't square or straight. Their accuracy was the best his table saws could attain, but well below my need for precision. His large-scale machines could have easily achieved my requirements, but either their precision wasn't something he noticed or he couldn't afford to maintain them. My instincts told me this.

Say you were a designer of model car kits. You sit in your office at Mattel and you design little Lamborghinis. You've designed a marvelous kit with clear instructions and all the pieces cut to exact specifications. You're proud of your creation. Would you now like to be held responsible for the successful construction of that model by a glue-squeezing, skateboard-riding, video-game-addicted, ten-year-old? No. Your plan is perfect and there is nothing that our little friend is going to add to your Lamborghini but the interesting effect of having the doors glued ajar.

Likewise, what architect wants to take responsibility for the actual construction of her project? In her mind, she can see her building and it is perfect. Why destroy that image with the reality of a job site strewn with sawdust, scrap wood, and garbage?

Some architects happily agree when the owners suggest that they save money by overseeing the construction themselves. The architect delivers a clean set of plans and walks away, leaving the owner to perform a double job—not only acting the role of the client as described in this book but also performing the role of architect, which involves overseeing and checking the quality of the contractor's work. The architect's job also involves interpreting the drawings and providing additional drawings and design services when the existing plans prove inadequate. These are chores that even the most seasoned architects find difficult.

Motivating the client's desire to take over the project is the fact that architects charge for this service, and most clients feel that since the plans are complete, there will be nothing for the architect to do but stand around and nod her head.

If the architect charges by the hour to visit the site, everyone watches the clock. If she includes oversight in her overall design package, the architect earns no additional money by coming (except artistic satisfaction). When paying work comes along, architects will make it their priority and the prepaid oversight will usually lapse.

Clients often combat this inattentiveness by inventing emergencies—calling the architect at ten at night to vent about some perceived problem: subcontractors, design, schedules, dust, etc. At the heart of these sometimes hysterical phone calls are legitimate problems that are inevitable to any custom product that the architect hasn't seen. She may even take the attitude that these problems are the contractor's fault. He contracted the job and the problems must be solved by him.

Another self-destructing way to save money is to not file the job with the city planning office. Filing the job probably means you have to hire an insured and licensed contractor who is much more expensive than the guy with two shovels and a beat-up Volvo. There will be a permit fee, and someone will inspect the plan and may reject elements of it or make other elements more expensive.

Most Americans agree that testing and approval are necessary, but drug companies, for example, are constantly lobbying for weaker regulations so they can sell their medicines to the public more quickly. Likewise, contractors would love to do away with regulations and permits because it slows them down.

The architect may argue for not filing as well, contending that she doesn't need the city's oversight (which may prevent her from doing what she really wants to do). However, the city is responsible for making sure buildings are safe and that they fit into the plan that the city as a whole has agreed to. While an architect or contractor may go along with an owner's wishes despite their better judgment, the city will have no misgivings about rejecting a plan they see as dangerous or against codes. For instance, "anti-backflow valves" prevent contaminated water from flowing back up through a faucet from an overflowing sink and into the city water supply. This valve may seem like a needless expense to you or be forgotten by your architect, but someday such a regulation could save a city a fatal epidemic. Look at California, where underengineered structures crumble during earthquakes. Though those unfiled renovations and their missing reinforcements and undersized beams save owners thousands of dollars in material and filing fees initially, they cost owners their houses and sometimes their lives during an earthquake.

Although I've been warning against the bad contractors of this world, only a small percentage of contractors are like Frank. Most are upstanding, hardworking men and women who want nothing more than to do a good job. But some owners think that deep beneath the well-referenced, seemingly reliable contractor is a scam artist. And many owners use this as an excuse to delay payments.

Withholding or delaying payments to the contractor can only slow the job while making things difficult for the contractor. It will also create resentment and fear for his subcontractors as they worry about getting paid.

During the initial construction phase, the contracted price may change due to three factors: *Extras* are those costs incurred when it becomes more costly to perform the work (e.g., when moving a sink it is discovered that the pipe in the wall is rotted and must be replaced). *Changes* are those additional costs caused by changing the plan (e.g., deciding to move the sink to a different wall, which will cause increases in plumbing, cabinet, and other related items). The third factor is problems caused by underbidding (e.g., forgetting there was a sink altogether).

These increases in the contracted price during the initial construction phase often damage the relationship among owners, architects, and contractors.

Extras caused by unknown conditions crop up as soon as you

begin demolition. Most likely, your contractor will find broken pipes or unknown structures that the owners pay for. If you spend $200 a day on extras for the first three days, it's very easy to imagine that your contractor will find extras *every* day.

It's also easy to imagine that these extras are not *real* problems, but a means by which the contractor can raise his price. Since he's already destroyed your kitchen, it seems he has you over a barrel. "Ma'am, we've opened up the walls and we can now see that your plumbing is rusted out. The pipes will have to be changed."

"Why didn't you see that before?" an owner will invariably ask.

"There was a wall there."

The second kind of additional cost is for changes. This is usually what happens when there is a change:

1. The owner doesn't understand the plans until the walls are actually raised.

2. Seeing the partially finished walls and not understanding the overall scheme of the architect, the client fears the worst. (Frequently, the owner has had one of his ideas shot down by the architect and has a score to settle.)

3. The owner insists the wall is wrong somehow and must be moved.

4. The contractor must now drop what he is doing and work out a plan to move this wall. All new electrical wire needs to be run, the ceiling lights must be moved, holes must be Spackled and the floor patched. All these things add extra costs to the entire project.

If the contractor submits a bill for moving the wall, the owners will likely refuse to pay and suggest the architect pay. A dispute will then ensue.

The third kind of extra cost is the most difficult to accept. It is the result of a job being underbid. This usually happens if you've hired the lowest bidder.

The lowest bidder has likely bid the job at exactly what he believes it will cost but has not factored in any unexpected costs. There are always going to be accidents: people cutting themselves or paint cans slipping; cutting off the wrong leg to level a table or ordering the wrong toilet. And there will be mistakes in the original bidding process like forgetting that electrical wires need to be removed from a wall before demolishing it.

A first-rate contractor has too much pride to complain about underbidding a section of work unless he can somehow pin it on the owner. The bargain contractor will not have allocated any money to emergencies, so that when the unexpected happens, he will either lose money or charge it to the owner as an "extra" and fight it out.

3

Solutions to Money Problems

First, listen to your instincts. With my cabinet nightmare in the previous chapter, I sensed a problem with the cabinetmaker's shop and I should have asked why he wasn't using the full-size panel saws instead of the little table saws. I also should have specified how important the squareness and straightness of the cabinets were to me and that he had to achieve this perfection with whatever tool he was using.

As an owner, you probably won't know about panel saws, but you will notice a messy work space and cheap machines. If things seem to be going wrong, pay attention. It's better to fire a contractor two days into the job than two months later when it's virtually impossible.

Frank's Volvo is a good indication that his financial resources were shaky. Past successes and recommendations are more important than a man's car, but you shouldn't ignore the obvious.

Next, pay your architect by the hour to come and inspect your job and be available for regular consultation to the contractor. Even the best designs will require quite a bit of hand-holding by the architect. Though you might think that you're paying the architect to stand around, it's money well spent.

Each type of extra requires a different strategy for the project to finish on time and on budget. For unknown conditions, your first line of defense will be the Rusk Bidding System in which the contractor makes holes in your walls to look for any existing problems.

After that, when previously unknown conditions crop up, do your best to have your contractor bid them at cost—especially since you paid the contractor to look for these things and he obviously missed them. Asking for cost means getting receipts. This might seem petty, but actually, if you don't request and subsequently receive the receipts after agreeing on cost, the contractor will feel stupid for not having upped the costs.

Review these unknown-condition problems with the architect and pay the contractor promptly for these extras once the architect authorizes them.

For extras caused by changes that the owner requests, the first line of defense is to examine the drawings thoroughly, get "renderings" (perspective drawings) if possible, and take on-site walkthroughs as often as possible to review how things are coming along. Next, try to make as few changes as possible. Weigh the advantage of the job being finished on time and within budget against the change you're requesting. It's impossible to make many changes and still come in on time and on budget. If you must make the change after construction has begun, have the contractor make a full bid on the cost of the change and how it affects the schedule of the entire project. Don't let the contractor start work without knowing these things. If owners who want to move a wall had to sign a change order for $2,100, they might be more willing to listen to the architect's reasons for the current room dimensions.

To protect against extras caused by underbidding, don't hire the lowest bidder unless you're sure he looked at the itemized bid of the consulting contractor and had taken all of the specifications into account.

If it turns out your contractor still underbid and needs more money, don't write him off. Work with the architect or a mediator to find out if his requests for more money are fair. You may want to remember what the other bidders were charging, to see what you would have paid for someone who anticipated all the details of the job. In most cases, you don't want to go much above the other contractors' prices unless it seems likely they underbid, too.

If it doesn't seem fair or right to pay the contractor more money, you may want to simply advance him money from the job to keep him going, although this is obviously risky, because the contractor could walk away with more money than you owe him, especially if the problems at the end of the job are bigger than your final payment. Your final payment, which is given after everything is complete, should never be less than 10 percent of the total job.

The first payment request will most likely be a dizzying compendium of numbers and will be difficult to decipher. Ask the contractor to review it with you. As much as you may like the contractor, tell him that money matters are serious and impersonal and that you will handle them that way. Look for areas in the bill in which the contractor is claiming he's completed more work than he has. At the same time, if the work has been done, don't hesitate to pay promptly. Keep the motor of construction fueled with money.

Beginning construction is often filled with unexpected problems, and as owner you are constantly asking the contractor for favors. Make deposits in the favor bank by paying fairly and as quickly as you feel comfortable. Later on when there are other problems, you will be able to say: "I've paid you promptly and I know you've appreciated that. Now I need a favor." A contractor's biggest fear, after plumbing leaks, is to not be paid for work done. An unpaid $20,000 bill can bankrupt a contractor. Your money negotiations should stress that you are looking for a fair deal that will never put either one of you at a fiscal disadvantage. Once the job begins, you'll want to reassure the contractor that he'll be paid everything he is owed. Withholding money, or giving the contractor any reason to doubt your word, is asking for trouble.

4

Time
Problems

Once a construction project begins, all things take twice as long. The reason for this is simple. When contractors estimate how long something will take, they're usually thinking how long it will take to do the work; but the "work" is only part of the time involved. For example, the work of putting up a Sheetrock closet might be four hours, but the time it will take to erect that closet is closer to eight or nine hours. That's because one has to pick up materials, get lunch, break a screw gun, call around to see if anyone has the parts to fix the screw gun, deal with workers that never show up, and so on.

Contractors constantly complain about how many problems there are on jobs, but many of them fail to realize that problems are the very essence of contracting—that they've been hired to solve the problems. If there were no problems in putting up a wall, then clients would do it themselves.

Interestingly, even though most owners know that there will be problems, when the contractor comes, the owners do everything they can to convince the contractors that the job is easy, and here's the surprise: *Most contractors believe it!*

Every day, contractors possessed of a sound mind and a healthy ego are pressured into believing that jobs are problem free. Worst of all, they are pressured by people who know nothing about construction. But problems inevitably surface and then the contractor is faced with these choices:

- Ignore the problem. This "solution" invariably causes worse problems later. Finding no stud in the wall to screw the cabinet to, the contractor in denial puts a lot of screws into the Sheetrock. Six months later, when the cabinets are filled with Grandmother's crystal, the cabinet falls.

- Fix the problem and absorb the cost. Rather than admit he hadn't checked to see if there were studs in the wall, he pretends he knew it all along in order to preserve his reputation, and installs grounds without charging for them.

- Make the client pay, and explain it as a "hidden condition."

Imagine this dilemma (ignore, pay, or charge) playing out twenty times a day. It causes money problems, but it also causes time problems. Many of these problems often don't take much more hardware—the material cost of opening up the wall and installing studs is negligible, but the cost in time will be relatively substantial and it will extend the project completion date.

The contractor again has choices:

- Ignore this increase in time and pretend that it will be made up later on.

- Note the increase in time, notify the client.

- Spend some extra money to hire more labor to compensate for the lost time. Hiring extra labor usually decreases efficiency and so it decreases profit for the contractor, especially if the contractor performs much of the work himself. Once a contractor has more than two helpers, his time will be spent talking to, supplying, and overseeing them.

Another big time drain is associated with the normal activities of life. Let's look at the eight-hour day of an average worker.

Punching in, discussing the previous night, changing clothes, getting instructions	**20 min**
Coffee break and getting reoriented to tasks	**22 min**
Getting job instructions throughout the day	**30 min**
Cleaning up job site before lunch	**10 min**
Lunch	**30 min**
Getting reoriented to tasks after lunch	**10 min**
Time on phone	**10 min**
Cleaning up at end of day	**30 min**

That's a total of two hours and forty-two minutes of time away from productive work. Multiply that by 5, and it's more than a day of the workweek spent not working.

Meanwhile, if a job starts running behind schedule, contractors think they'll be able to pound nails themselves to catch up, which is completely ridiculous. Their day is filled with picking things up at supply houses, making at least two hours of calls a day, straightening out things with the client and the architect, selling new jobs, taking care of problems on previous and other jobs, and taking care of family business. Once your job starts to run over schedule, it's difficult to make up time.

5

Solutions to Time Problems

I f in construction everything takes twice as long as it should, how is it possible to stay on schedule?

You must constantly reassert control over time or it will control you. Never ignore that the project is falling behind—immediately note it and demand a course correction from the contractor. The contractor must keep the job site manned with enough people, and he must get his material and equipment ordered ahead of time. The architect must constantly feed needed information to the owner and the contractor, and the owner must avoid making unnecessary changes.

The schedule is the tool for controlling your job and for making sure that the contractor adheres to his commitments. This schedule must be reviewed constantly. I can't tell you how many times I've been in the middle of a job and thought I was on schedule when the client requested an updated schedule, and I discovered that I had completely forgotten an entire part of the job.

If a job is on schedule and a major change is made, the schedule often isn't refigured and the job will drift off. Likewise, if a "hidden condition" problem develops, the contractor may try to lump all his inefficiencies on a broken pipe. For both changes and hidden conditions, you must immediately ask the contractor for a fair and substantiated change to the schedule and then make it clear that you expect the contractor to follow this new schedule.

Request that the weekly revised schedule be posted at the job site and never accept a "no schedule" situation.

Knowing the schedule will save wear and tear on your nerves as you watch the work progress. The demolition phase of the job goes very quickly, but the actual construction gets slower and slower as the work progresses. If you don't have a reliable schedule to follow, your concern about the job falling behind—even if it's not—might get on the contractor's nerves and that will certainly slow him down.

You must let the contractor know that you respect his schedule and that you'll do everything you can to help him stay on schedule. The contractor is constantly faced with this choice: save money and fall behind schedule or lose money and stay on schedule. You must always try to convince the contractor that he is not allowed to fall behind schedule; that he will have to either spend the money or plan better.

If you've already decided on a complete plan, problems will occur less frequently. Though you may visit or call the job site once a day to make sure the contractor or supervisor is there, a weekly meeting is a better way to keep track of everything. At these meetings the architect, contractor, and owner should review the schedule, any change orders, progress payments, questions, and problems. Once-a-week meetings with all the participants will save time and ensure that progress continues.

The architect must still be available to the contractor by phone daily. Throughout every job the contractor usually has at least a few questions for the architect every day. Some of these questions relate to things that aren't on the blueprints: "What kind of doorknobs do you want?" Some of these questions relate to things that may have been overlooked: "I spoke to the plumber and he says if the counter is that low on the island, he can't run a vent pipe. What do you want to do?" Some of these questions relate to problems in procuring materials: "The Porcher toilet won't be in stock for a month. Do you want to wait or do you want to get something else?"

These questions will always come up. If there is no line of communication between the contractor and the architect, the job might stay on schedule, but you'll get the contractor's quickest and cheapest alternative. Of course, there is nothing wrong with cheap, simple alternatives, but it's the architect's job to see the whole picture. Only she knows that the bathroom was designed around the Porcher toilet and that without that shapely European bowl the bathroom's design won't make sense.

An open line of communication between the contractor and the design professional will yield rapid decisions that follow the spirit of the project. The design professional understands the overall project in a context of time and money better than an owner is able to.

6

Power
Problems

As the construction stage begins, your relationship with your contractor will change. Until now, he has given you valuable advice, researched prices, and provided a negotiated contract. When the work begins, you might find your contractor covered in plaster dust, carrying a broken toilet out to his truck. As good as actual construction work might feel to the contractor, this change in position—from professional to worker—may bother him, especially when the architect or owner is around.

Construction sites offer primitive comforts. Toilets are makeshift, and lunch facilities might consist of an overturned joint-compound bucket for a chair and a couple of sawhorses for a table. An elegant client coming by can hurt sensitive egos.

As bad as it is for the contractor, it can be worse for the workers and craftsmen. For some reason, some people (whether client, architect, or designer) have a tendency to treat the craftsman disrespectfully.

Two of the best molding installers I've ever met had become sickened by the constant interruption and complaint of the client. Finally, while installing egg and dart molding in the bathroom, they fashioned a tribute to this particular client. On the most prominent outside corner they brought two eggs of the molding together and formed a perfect little permanent buttocks.

Before the job begins, it is the architect and the client who spend the most time together. But once the work begins, the contractor will spend much more time with the client. This creates jealousy and mistrust between the architect and the contractor, which often leads to backbiting that can ruin the project.

7

Solutions to
Power Problems

For some reason, contractors and architects brush off compliments, and yet we relish them and so do the people who work for us. Those clients who rave about our workmanship often get even better workmanship, a more beautiful job, and *a more pleasant construction experience*. (It's my belief that if you're spending $30,000 and three months of your life on something, you should enjoy it.) Contractors go all out for these appreciative clients because they want to get more praise. If a contractor has a reputation for quality, he will want to preserve it. For a contractor, that reputation is money in the bank.

Raving about your contractor's work isn't particularly helpful if you're constantly making changes, resisting decisions, or running out of money. Your job will turn into a time and fiscal nightmare—but, incredibly, you'll probably still get a top-quality job from your contractor.

Find out what's good about the contractor's work and praise it. In this way you will bolster the confidence of the contractor and ease that transition from white-collar owner to blue-collar worker. It's often helpful to think of a skilled contractor as an artisan.

Learn the names of the people on the job site, introduce yourself, and take an interest in them. They will be more likely to do a good job knowing that they are not anonymous, that the client knows which door they hung.

Most craftsmen could earn more money in another profession. What often motivates them is the desire to create and to be appreciated for that creation.

Finally, bring by friends and acquaintances to see the work, especially people who are thinking of hiring a contractor to do work on their homes.

8

Management Problems

Construction is difficult work.

Small contractors (the type you'll probably hire for home renovations) often have a difficult time managing projects once they've started. Most small contractors start their careers as single carpenters doing jobs by themselves. As they become more experienced and get bigger jobs, they are able to hire additional help, but the people they hire probably aren't as skilled as the contractor or they would be too expensive to afford. As the projects get larger, the contractor needs to spend more time maintaining a schedule, ordering material, generating change orders, and overseeing workers. This means that the contractor spends less time doing the carpentry that he's good at and more time managing the project.

This tortures the contractor as he watches carpenters less competent than he is work slowly away at the job while he makes phone calls. The contractor who succumbs too often to this torture will strap on his nail bag and jump in, pushing the job along beautifully until it grinds to a halt for lack of materials, subcontractors, and money.

Another problem for contractors is control and management of subcontractors. The contractor will most likely hire subcontractors to execute much of the work on the job, from excavation to plumbing, electric, framing, Sheetrock, ceilings, cabinets, and paint. Though the contractor you've hired probably qualifies as a small business, the subcontractors he hires may be much larger companies. The electrical contractor, for instance, is a licensed company and will likely have much larger projects than installing kitchen outlets at your house. If that electrical subcontractor needs to meet a deadline on a $50,000 municipal lighting job, he will pull his electricians off your job no matter what your contractor says. In many ways, these subcontractors are beyond the direct control of your contractor.

Changes requested by clients create another management problem for contractors. Contractors often don't inform owners of the extra cost and time of a change because (1) they don't really know how much the changes will cost or how much it will affect the schedule, (2) they are in too much of a rush to sit down and figure it out, and (3) they want to be thought of as the kind, generous contractor and are afraid that if they present extras, especially as they multiply, the owner will be angry.

Sometimes owners allow themselves to stay uninformed because they're hoping that they'll never be charged for these extras. They believe that since the job has run on too long, or that the contractor made some mistakes, or that the contractor is sympathetic to the owners having spent so much money, the contractor will forgive all the extras.

The final management problem arises from the contractor's reaction to adversity. Our contractor is human, and when problems come up, he gets upset. When he sees that the job will go on longer, that he will make less profit, that things won't look as good, or that the client is upset, he may:

- Redouble his effort

- Smoke several cigarettes and drink coffee in the hope that his brain will be stimulated

- Have a drink

- Have a sandwich

- Take a walk around the block

- Get busy with something else that's less complicated and forget about the whole problem

- Keel over with a heart attack

All of these responses will relieve stress, but some aren't in your project's best interest.

The architect's management problems will start after she's finished making all the drawings and reading all the contracts and has put off all her other projects to get yours off the ground. Your job starts and she focuses in on her other projects only to have the inevitable early construction problems of dimensions not lining up and hidden conditions demanding her attention back at your job. She will obviously be resistant to leaving her other projects to return again to yours.

Owners, who seemed to have so many decisions to make during the design phase, suddenly have time on their hands and often create management problems for themselves. Those who haven't had the privilege of reading this book won't know what to do and will start making changes, fretting about the inadequacy of the personnel on the job, and getting in the way of progress. This, dear reader, fortunately won't happen to you.

9

Solutions to Management Problems

Incredibly, you are able to solve management problems for your contractor and architect by making rules and enforcing them.

The first step to effective management is to enforce weekly meetings so you can:

- Go over all problems and changes

- Receive change orders with prices and adjustments to the completion date

- Review the revised schedule

- Tour the job site to inspect the location of walls, doorways, lights, switches, and outlets

- Inspect the quality of the work with the architect's help

- Receive pay requests

- Praise good work

- Demand explanations for bad work and schedule its correction. If there is bad work, this tone must be set immediately to avoid larger problems later.

- Discuss the project in private with the architect before and after the meeting. Just as the contractor was objective during the design phase, the architect will now be able to note where things are going awry.

Make a brief phone call to the job daily to make sure the contractor or his super is on the job and to find out if things are going well.

One solution to the problem of subcontractors abandoning your job when other jobs call is to introduce yourself to the master electrician, the master plumber, and whoever else is working for the contractor. Let them know why your job will be a "trophy job," why it's important to be on time and on budget, and that you value quality work—especially when it comes to making sure that things are centered and level.

When the electrician has to choose between not showing up at the $50,000 commercial job or your job, he'll always go to the commercial job for the day. But by your actions, your personal introductions, your insistence on quality, and your lack of changes, you may at least get him to forsake another residential project for yours when the choice comes up.

If you've done as I've suggested throughout the book so far and fully developed your plan and worked it into your budget, now is the time to relax and put all your work into getting that plan beautifully built. It's easy to want to change, to do something else creative. Don't. If things don't look quite right now, it's probably because they're not finished.

After you've finished the design and contracting phases, the key to having a successful renovation is to stick to the plan.

10

Quality Problems

Biblically, "The seed sown on shallow soil is sure to falter." For construction, the finished quality of the job lies in the beginning of construction. If you wait until the dropped ceiling is hung and painted and all the cabinets are finally installed to notice that the ceiling is wavy (it will only be obvious once the cabinets are installed near the ceiling), it will be very difficult—if not impossible—to correct. Yes, it's the contractor's fault, but you need to ask yourself if you want the contractor to rip the entire job apart and set aside another month for construction.

The problem would be evident after the walls are initially framed with studs and before the plasterboard has gone up. This stage is called rough framing, and I think this nomenclature gets everyone in trouble. In the old days, studs were uneven and covered with wood strips (lath) to hold the plaster. They would be crooked but the plasterer would come along and even everything out. Today, Sheetrock is attached directly to the studs, and if the studs aren't exactly plumb, the Sheetrock won't be plumb either. That's not apparent when you look at a wall, but when you try to hang double doors on that wall, the two doors will probably be even at the top but one will stick out three-quarters of an inch at the bottom. Likewise, if you hang a cabinet on such a wall, it's likely the doors will be crooked and bind.

Rough framing isn't often checked by architects and owners at the beginning of construction because everyone is busy acting pleasant and positive. The contractor looks competent and everyone assumes that if the walls are crooked, it is the contractor's problem. It will be his problem, but it will be yours as well.

Architects also miss problems of quality of work because they often come to job sites dressed well and can't be climbing over bags of cement and dusty two-by-fours to check the walls. The only way to inspect quality is to narrow one's eyes and look straight at it.

Sometimes, architects hope that by hiring the right contractor they won't have to worry about quality. Contractors need oversight.

11

Solutions to Quality Problems

Contractors want to give a better job than they can deliver.

Before the work starts, you can only get them to make so many promises. But when work begins, you must speak immediately, in private, to the contractor about what you like and don't like on the job. This course is vital to getting the best-quality work. On the first day of the renovation, come home midday to see if:

- The furniture is properly covered and the work area is sealed off

- Tools aren't lying on furniture or other easily damaged surfaces

- Building materials and debris are organized

- Proper lighting is in place for the workers

Contractors will have a limited amount of time to prepare a work area for the construction that is to follow. If you see that preparation work isn't being done, remind the contractor of the amount of money allotted in his bid for general conditions and protection.

You can make things easier for the contractor by moving furniture and other personal items from the work area and by arranging a place for the contractor to store materials, debris, and tools. Set up a place for the workers to keep their lunch, and provide a list of the local hardware, lumber, and paint stores, as well as the hospital, the deli, and every possible way to get in touch with you.

Whatever you do to save the contractor time will result in a better job for you.

The weekly meeting is crucial to developing quality. At the first meeting (probably at the end of demolition) ask the contractor to show you what he's proud of and how a shoddy contractor would have done the work differently. It will be interesting for you, increase your understanding of the job, and establish that you expect quality, that you are *inspecting* for quality, and that you appreciate quality.

Ask what he will be doing for the next week and what to look for at the next meeting.

Treat the contractor as a competent craftsman throughout the job and let your role be the positive, curious client with a fussy architect in tow. If you let the contractor educate you about quality, he won't be able to ignore the quality of your renovation. His pride will force him to do the best job possible.

Often some final design elements aren't settled by the start of construction. You must maintain quality of design as you approach demolition. These final decisions will determine the design quality of your house. The light fixtures, the door hardware, even the microwave. Pay attention to these details.

Here's a handy checklist to post at the job site. It's a kind of report card for the contractor. Consult it each week as you walk through the job. Seeing it posted will ensure that everyone does the right job for you.

General

- Are floors protected?

- Is the job site, including bathroom, clean?

- Are tools orderly?

- Is trash properly disposed of?

Carpentry

- Are rooms the right size?

- Are walls plumb and straight?

- Are doorways big enough?

- Do doors fit their openings properly?

- Are dropped ceiling lines straight?

- Do moldings have tight corners with little, if any, fill?

Electric

- Are light switches in the right place?

- Are there enough outlets and are they in the right place?

- Are lights centered?

- Are heights of outlets and switches consistent?

Plumbing

- Do drain lines have the proper pitch?

- Do supply lines have antihammer columns?

- Are fixtures centered?

- Are fixtures damaged, marred, or scratched?

- Are there any leaks?

Cabinetwork

- Do doors and countertops align?

- Is fill in woodwork visible?

- Are corners sharp and defined?

- Do all drawers and doors work well?

- Is finish even and consistent?

- Is anything damaged or marred?

- Does the cabinetwork conform to the plan?

Tile work

- Are the lines in the tile work straight and consistent in width?

- Are the planes of tile flat?

- Is the grout consistent in depth and color?

- Are the tile faces perfectly clean of grout and glue?

- Are cut edges smooth?

- Are the tiles lined up so they are centered between walls and with no pieces less than a half tile at the edges?

Paint

- Are the walls smooth with no joints apparent?

- Was a bonding agent used for plaster repairs? (If so, is there telltale blue or pink paint around repairs?)

- Was tape used for cracks? (You'll only notice this early in the work.)

- Is woodwork free of drips and heavy brush marks?

- Are walls free of heavy roller marks and runs?

- Are lines of two adjoining colors sharp?

- Is there paint dripped or spattered on hinges, floors, plumbing fixtures, etc.?

Floors

- Have door thresholds been replaced as needed?

- Are floors repaired as needed?

- Have squeaks been addressed?

- Is the floor free of sanding marks and dips?

- Is the floor smooth and dust free?

- Is the staining even and consistent?

If you discover a part of the work that is not done well, ask that it be corrected as soon as possible. Doing this early on will make the contractor reluctant to do anything else that is slipshod. One of my favorite customers once found some bad tile work about halfway into the job. He was nice about it: "I was surprised to see this. The tiles must have slipped after you'd gone home for the day." But he made it clear that I was to reset them. I had to tear out about nine square feet of tile to fix the problem, and we both felt much better about it.

The Finleys—
Setting the
Machine in
Motion

Tom Finley looked at the clock in the kitchen. He felt like he was back in high school and deciding whether or not to invite Sue Cote to the prom.

"You know, Tom," Michelle said, "if you don't call him soon, he's going to be in bed."

"But I hate to call him at his house."

"He works out of his house."

Tom sighed. "So I'm just asking when to expect him."

"Yes, ask him when, realistically, he should be here. We want to start this right."

"Why don't you call him?"

"Fine," Michelle said. "You're such a wus." She started for the phone book.

"Okay, I'll call. You give me the number."

"I'll call."

"Just give me the number."

Michelle gave him a look that only worried him, then called out the number.

"Hello, Mr. DeTomaso? . . . Tom Finley. How are you? . . . Just wanted to know when you'd be by tomorrow . . . Yes, I put up the plastic drop cloths . . . No, I figured you wouldn't be here right at eight . . . Right, get the tools, materials. I just wanted to make sure everything started out all right. Michelle's teaching tomorrow morning . . . Nine o'clock is good. I'll hold you to that . . . See you then . . . Our check cleared, right? . . . Very good. Good night.

"I sounded like an idiot, Michelle."

"You did but I love you just the same. Asking about the check was good, though, and you were nicely polite—yet firmish."

The truck pulled up at 8:50 and Tom fairly sailed down the steps to greet it. "Mr. DeTomaso. How are things?"

"Very well. It's not a problem I'm early?"

"No, not in the least. Can I help you in with things?"

"No, first I want to come in and see how your drop clothes are."

Tom backed up a little as DeTomaso went in to inspect the house.

"Didn't they have the big sheets of plastic where I sent you?"

Tom smiled a funny smile as he looked at the sheets of plastic he had taped together. "Mr. DeTomaso, my guess is that you know full well I didn't go where you sent me."

"Next time you do. I don't like the tape. It comes apart and then you holler at me about the dust."

"I can retape it."

"Good, my son will give you duct tape. Both sides." DeTomaso looked around a bit more. "Okay, Leonardo," he yelled out to the truck. "Bring in the Masonite. We put the tools here."

His son brought in the Masonite and Mr. DeTomaso spent the next half hour arranging his tools very neatly on the Masonite. He then set up a desk, plugged a portable phone into a phone jack, and taped the plans, the schedule, and a list of phone numbers on the wall.

"These are all the possible ways to get ahold of me," DeTomaso said. "Beeper, cell phone, home number. Any problem, you get ahold of me—but say I'm gone off the planet and we spring a leak. Here's the plumber, the electrician, and my son's number. Only in emergency, correct, Mr. Finley?"

"Very good. That's good."

"Now, where is the closest hospital with an emergency room, God forbid."

"Straight up Utica on the left a quarter mile."

"Your number at work, Mr. Finley?" as he wrote onto the contact sheet.

Tom gave him the number and, at DeTomaso's request, his wife's as well.

"And the designer, Chris whatever."

"You should have the number."

"You're right, Mr. Finley, but I'm very lazy."

Tom smiled, looked at the bottom of the plans, and gave him Chris's number.

"You're very smart, Mr. Finley. As smart as I am lazy. We're done now. You've seen us get set up. Now leave us to work and don't think any more about us."

Tom looked at DeTomaso. "Are you kicking me out?"

"Yes, and don't stop by unless you have to. We have work to do, and when you're around I have to be nice to my son and polite in general."

Tom nodded awkwardly. "Uh, well. Very well. I'll be going."

"Yes, you must make the money to pay me. Very important, Mr. Finley. Very important."

Tom backed out and realized Mr. DeTomaso had just taken over the job.

As Michelle drove up after work, she could see that someone had delivered a large Dumpster and placed it in the driveway. Otherwise, there was no sign that anything had happened during the day. She opened the back door into the kitchen, where the first thing she noticed was Mr. DeTomaso's vacuum cleaner. He had broken through into the study as planned—the plastic was a little opaque with dust, but he had put down Masonite on the floor and everything looked very tidy and clean. His tools were lined up. Michelle couldn't quite believe it. There was a note: "Everything OK. May not have mentioned the Dumpster, my apologies. No surprises so far except one pipe is shot. I'll give you price over the phone tomorrow."

Chris Layner drove through the scrubbed neighborhood to the house, the setting sun giving everything an orange tint.

The neighborhood had changed in her mind now. No longer was it some other architect's neighborhood that she was critiquing; this would be her neighborhood and she now looked at it appraisingly to see what needed to be done.

She had visited the site once already when Mr. DeTomaso laid out the lines on the floor for the walls two days before. Since then, he had told her he had studded out all the walls and had his electrician install the boxes for the ceiling lights, the switches and outlets, and had his plumber do all the rough connections.

They had spoken at least every day and he had called more than a few times on the first couple of days with questions about how things went together and such.

DeTomaso brought out the level with a flourish. "Other carpenters they wouldn't do this but I do. Now when they ask you why you spend so much for Giovanni, you don't say 'I don't know.'"

The level knocked against the wood stud. DeTomaso's eyes flared slightly as he looked at the level, then slid it up the straight stud. He flipped the level over as the Finleys and Chris Layner watched him.

It was Tom who broke the silence. "So we pay Mr. DeTomaso so much money so he can make the walls crooked for us?"

"Leonardo," Mr. DeTomaso called. "Bring me the Wonderbar and a sledgehammer and a hammer and tenpenny nails." This was said in such a passionate way that he could have been screaming expletives and they would have sounded just the same. As Tom, Michelle, and Chris watched, DeTomaso pulled out the nails in the wall, moved it, plumbed it, nailed it, and held the level up to the audience. "Plumb! . . . Now, lest I drive myself to destruction, allow me to check the rest of the walls and God have mercy on my son's soul."

DeTomaso went over the rest of the walls, banged one wall over a bit, and slammed in another nail but otherwise approved. He then took Mrs. Finley around and showed her the now centered bubble in the level. "You see, everywhere else I do a nice job."

"Yes, Mr. DeTomaso, I can see that."

"It is my son—he thinks of the girls, he thinks of Naples, he forgets what a plumb bob is, and he thinks that his eye is as good as his papa's. It is not. What do you think of our outlets?"

Mrs. Finley, who was finding herself amused by Mr. DeTomaso, looked at Tom. "Tom, how are the outlets?"

"What should I be looking for?"

Chris broke in, "Up to now you've been looking at a plan. Now you can see where the outlets really are. The question, really, is are there enough and where are you planning on putting your furniture?"

"Well," Michelle said. "Is there room for a little shelf or something to put keys and mail when we come in?"

Chris said, "You mentioned that before and I was thinking we could have a little cherry shelf like the rest of the cabinets with a little light over the top of it."

DeTomaso rolled his eyes. "A shelf is easy, electric is getting more complex. How much you want to hold up the job to do this?"

"Mr. DeTomaso," Chris said quickly, "let's see how many changes in total we're considering. I agree, if we start moving everything around, it will delay the job, but this is the only change I was thinking about on the way to this meeting."

Tom said, "I have one of those cordless screwdrivers. We didn't think of someplace where I could plug that in."

"Oh, honey." Michelle rolled her eyes. "I was trying to think of something to put over the kitchen table. That's it—an outlet with your screwdriver plugged into it."

"Mrs. Finley," DeTomaso said, "a man has a right to a cordless screwdriver. Where do you keep it now, Mr. Finley?"

"In the garage."

"Perfect."

Now it was Michelle's turn. "This is funny, but how about my Dustbuster?"

"I don't think you want that over the kitchen table either," DeTomaso said. "Seriously, you have that cordless hand mixer, too. Could we put some outlets in a cabinet somewhere?"

Chris looked unhappy. "I'm sorry I didn't think of those things. You really use them?"

"All the time," Michelle said. "And where's the phone?"

"The phone is here," Chris said.

"Where's the outlet?" Tom said.

Chris looked very unhappy. "You have a cordless phone."

"It's the twentieth century," Tom said.

"We need one outlet strip, in a cabinet with a shelf beside it for a cordless phone," DeTomaso said, pointing and gesturing with his hands. "Inside, plug-in doohickeys, very convenient. Outside, cordless phone, antenna in space, easy to charge up phone. Better yet, mount the phone on the sidewall of the cabinet. Ms. Layner, where would you suggest?"

"Thank you, Giovanni, I was thinking the same thing. How about right here by the door, this cabinet. We extend the shelf a little and keys can be here and mail. Perhaps a little messy with the phone, everything all in one."

"Where do I write when I'm on the phone?" Tom asked.

"It's a cordless so wherever you want," DeTomaso said. "But put a little pad on the shelf, too. And you don't need the little light. It's light enough here. Is this resolved?"

"Let me think about it, but yes, it sounds good," Chris said. "I'll give the go-ahead after we've all thought about it overnight. Now, is the location for the hanging lamp over the table right?"

"Excuse me for interrupting, but have you got the table yet for in here?" DeTomaso asked.

"You'll be using the same table, right?"

Tom and Michelle nodded.

"Leonardo, bring in the table and the chairs for us."

Leonardo brought in the table, and after pushing it around they decided the ceiling lamp would be better moved over a foot. "This is why you hire Giovanni. See the slack in the wire? I put it there so if, God forbid, I have to move it, I do it easily. I charge fifteen dollars."

"Fifteen dollars?" Tom said.

"If I no think ahead and new wire had to be run, it would be thirty-five. I save you money, I make some too. Otherwise, why should I be so smart?"

"So now let us talk about money," Chris Layner said. "Did you have a chance to look over the payment request?"

Tom nodded. "We were confused, though, about what was actually done. We thought we'd ask you."

"Quite right," Chris said. "Everything looked fine except where it says that the plumbing is seventy percent complete. That seems high."

DeTomaso nodded. "It always seems high to me, too, but look at what the plumber's done. He hook up the water and the vent and the waste for the sink, he run the line for the dishwasher, he has the line for the refrigerator. All the materials and labor."

"But aren't the plumbing fixtures part of that number as well? They haven't been delivered. They make up more than fifty percent of the plumbing cost."

DeTomaso's face turned bright red in an instant as he looked at the bid. "I'm afraid I make a mistake. You right. I have ordered them. But you right, I don't pay until they come. My apologies."

"No problem, Mr. DeTomaso," Michelle said. "I don't think it was intentional. So where are we on the pay request, then?"

Chris smiled. "Well, incidentally, it doesn't matter about the plumbing because Mr. DeTomaso did a thousand dollars more than the value of this payment request and the plumbing deduction would only be about six hundred and fifty, so he's still fine. Now the extras. Here is the change order for the replacement of the cold-water pipe. How did you get this number, Mr. DeTomaso?"

"This is what my plumber charge me plus my overhead."

"Which is?"

"Twenty-five percent. That covers oversight, warrantee, overhead, cleaning up, and profit."

Chris looked at the Finleys. "We really should have agreed on a percentage for Mr. DeTomaso beforehand."

DeTomaso bowed his head. "I only charge twenty-five percent, never more, never less. Next time we work together I'll mention it in my bid."

Tom said, "That's fine. Really, things seem to be going very well here, we're glad we found a way to afford you. If this amount here at the bottom is correct, I'll give you a check now or I could wire the money into your account tomorrow."

"You do that?" DeTomaso asked.

"If you need the money, I will do it."

"Thank you," DeTomaso said. "Very good. Anything else?"

"No, I'm sure you'd like to get home and see your family."

DeTomaso agreed and left quickly, leaving the Finleys and Chris Layner standing in the kitchen.

"How do you think things look, Chris?" Tom asked.

"Things look very good."

"Then thank you, too. We have a bill from you, right, Chris?"

"Yes."

"Then let's pay that now."

Beginning Construction Checklist

Money

- Look for the contractor's money problems.
- Try to get "extras" at cost, since your contractor has investigated existing conditions for a fee.
- Go over pay requests carefully.
- Keep your design person on payroll.
- Pay promptly.

Time

- Be aware of how precious the contractor's time is and don't waste it with useless requests.
- Make sure the contractor knows how precious your time is and don't allow him to waste it with sloppy management.
- Review schedules at the weekly meetings.
- Post the schedule.

Power

- Treat the contractor and the people who work with him well.
- Learn the names of people on the job site, call them by name, and acknowledge their work.
- Bring friends who are considering work of their own.

Management

- Use the weekly meeting to control your job.
- Arrange for your architect's availability by phone and in person for the contractor.
- Insist all change orders are written and priced ahead of the work commencing.
- Scrutinize the updated time schedule for problems the contractor is overlooking.

- Use the acrhitect for objective criticism during construction, just as you used the contractor for objective criticism during design.
- Ask the contractor to make mock-ups of walls and counters using Masonite or cardboard to assist everyone in visualizing the finished architectural relationships e.g., is the proposed closet too big?
- Walk through the job site with the contractor and architect after the framing is complete to check that the walls are in their best location, and again after the electrical roughing is done to make sure switches, ceiling fixtures, etc., are all in the correct locations. I advocate against change, but now's the time to do it if you've made a mistake.
- Use daily phone calls to keep people on the job.
- Keep a log of extras, payments.

Quality

- Ask the contractor to demonstrate the quality of his work and to explain what to look for the following week.
- Ask how shoddy contractors would do the same work.
- Ask the architect to reevaluate the plan as the work progresses.
- Make and maintain a quality checklist on the job so all trades know what standard they are being judged by.

Part Four

Ending
Construction

1

The Hamptons— the Completion of a Nightmare Kitchen

Cindy sat in her office at the hotel daydreaming about her kitchen. Finally today, four and a half months since they started, Frank was installing her cabinets. The walls and new ceiling were up, plastered and painted. The plumbing and electric were in. The door frames for the closets were in and the doors were beside them. All Frank said he had to do was throw in the cabinets and countertops, hook up the plumbing and the appliances, put in the doors they'd added, and then install the new vinyl floor.

It seemed like a lot to Cindy, but Frank had said getting the framework in was the hard part. The finishing touches were easy.

The framework had been tough. The steel beam that bisected their kitchen was enormous. It hung down a foot and a half from the ceiling and was wrapped in Sheetrock. Cindy was glad that she wasn't paying for it.

•   •   •

Sour sweat was pouring off of Frank.

Somehow, either he had mismeasured the cabinets at the beginning of the job or he had mismeasured the door, and now the cabinets protruded about four inches past the entrance to the next room. All the cabinets had drawers in them so he couldn't cut them down. He would have to cut the extra length out of the sink cabinet.

Or they could buy new cabinets, but Frank was sure that Cindy would end up making him pay for those.

Frank didn't like to saw things up on the job. The wood could splinter, the cuts might waver, you could make a mistake . . .

He started to gag on the smell of his own sweat.

Then the answer came to him. The difficult cut would be the doors. But those he could take over to a friend's cabinet shop. He could tell Mrs. Hampton he wanted to leave the doors off so they would be protected while the final work was done.

Frank removed the bottom cabinets quickly and using his jigsaw started cutting off the four inches. He cut from the back forward. Unfortunately for the front face of the cabinet, Frank's jigsaw blade was dull, forcing him to use more pressure than he should have. When he had almost cut through to the front face of the cabinet, the remaining veneer of dark wood splintered out on either side of the cut, revealing the white particleboard carcass underneath.

But Frank couldn't see the front of the cabinet where he had been cutting. He didn't notice the splinter of dark wood as he swept away the sawdust and debris, and so lost any chance of gluing it back on.

When the Hamptons pulled into their driveway, they were slightly surprised not to see Frank's Volvo there, especially tonight when they knew he would be having a hard time finishing the cabinets. Cindy had made it a special point to get him to make promises, because that seemed to be the only thing that kept him going. She had raised holy hell whenever he didn't finish what he said he would. Frank's wife had even called her two days ago, begging Cindy to let Frank come home at a more reasonable hour.

As Larry pulled the groceries out of the car, Cindy ran ahead to see what had happened inside. She came out, thrilled. "Larry, he actually did it. The cabinets are up. You've got to see it. Come."

As Larry unloaded the groceries Cindy came down the driveway holding a note. "He says he's very concerned about protecting the cabinets from damage, so he's storing the doors away from the cabinets and he's covered all the cabinets with masking tape and paper. But look. It looks like a kitchen."

In fact, it did. The cabinets circled the room. There were no countertops yet because Frank was making those up himself to save some money. But he had kept his word about the cabinets.

In the next two weeks, Frank installed the countertops, also protected by paper and tape. The lighting fixtures went in and the appliances were installed. Frank even seemed to pick up the pace after the Hamptons paid him 75 percent of the total job since it was obvious he was almost finished. He tiled the sink backsplash as an extra and then, finally, laid down the floor. That was Thursday. All that was left to install were the cabinet doors. Then the Hamptons could fire up their new kitchen.

Mr. Nostrami stood in the center of the kitchen. "I do not know why you did not call me before. This is an abomination. Have you had work done before?"

Cindy was trying to compose her face but it was twitching. Larry was holding his mouth very tight.

Mr. Nostrami continued, "You did not see the work as he was going along?"

Larry's voice was tight. "He was protecting things as he went along. He didn't want anything to get damaged. He wrapped everything with paper. I could see that there were tiles up, but I couldn't see that the spaces between the tiles didn't match up."

"Who was the subcontractor who installed these tiles?"

"I think this was all Frank," Cindy said.

"No," Mr. Nostrami said. "Frank was the contractor. Who actually did all this work?"

"That's what I'm saying," Cindy said. "This was all Frank."

"What is under the floor?" Mr. Nostrami asked, leaning down to catch the light bouncing off the floor. "It looks like he didn't even sweep."

Larry spoke. "Well, when he laid down the floor it looked flat."

"That is because the tile is still rigid, but as you walk on it, it conforms to the subsurface." Mr. Nostrami looked at the ceiling. "Look around this light here. Do you see how the light shows all the imperfections in the ceiling? Without the light and painted flat you don't see it, but now with the light you can see he didn't sand many places."

Cindy nodded. "Yes, we are aware of that. Do you know if these cabinet doors can be adjusted?"

"How do you mean? These are traditional face frame cabinets. As long as they are set level, they never need to be adjusted." Mr. Nostrami looked now at the cabinets. His face went blank and one could almost hear his stomach turning, his displeasure was so great. "This man is an idiot."

Every door hung crooked against the next one. Along the countertops, there was a quarter of an inch step between one piece and the next, with an eighth-inch gap between the two countertops.

The door that Frank had cut down had not turned out well. When Frank had conceived of the idea, he was thinking they were flat doors. In fact, they were raised panel doors, so to cut off four inches left a door without an edge frame. It was like cutting four inches off a painting, leaving one end of the canvas flopping in the breeze. Because he had chopped down the sink cabinet, the sink was not only off center, but it extended into the next cabinet, which had a series of drawers. As a result, the top two drawers couldn't be opened.

Mr. Nostrami asked, "How much have you paid Frank?"

"About seventy-five percent of his bill."

"You have a problem on your hands."

Now it was Cindy's turn. "Mr. Nostrami, Frank brought you into this project. If his work was inadequate, you had a responsibility to inform us of that."

"Mrs. Hampton, you never asked me to come to inspect the work. I drew the beam for you, I got your building department inspection. I have not even been paid for my second invoice. I assumed everything was going well until you called me last night at ten o'clock."

"Mr. Nostrami, it was a conflict of interest for you to—"

"This is a business of cooperation!"

"Don't raise your voice to me! You did not monitor the work!"

"Because you didn't want to pay the seventy-five dollars an hour, Mrs. Hampton!"

That hurt because it was true. Everything did seem fine, and inviting this man over to say the same thing for $75 seemed a waste of time. The comment stopped Cindy in her tracks so that when her voice came again it was low and guttural. "My lawyer will look at that, just as he will look at your contract and your relationship with Frank. To come in now and pick at his work when obviously you had to know the kind of contractor he was suggests that there was a conflict of interest. As I understand your business, you work for the *client*, but here you were staying away so that Frank could get paid and there would be no problems. This kitchen has to be redone and I am not paying for it." Cindy had spoken, her mind made up. She turned on her heel and walked away.

Larry stood looking at Nostrami. But there were no more comments to make for either one of them, so Mr. Nostrami gathered his bag and went out without another word.

When Frank's countersuit came in, the Hamptons were shocked. Frank was suing them for the value of his extras, which amounted to over $10,000, including the beam. He was suing them for the month delay when they didn't have the building permit. And he was suing them for something called cardinal change, which meant that things had changed so much from the original plan that, in fact, the Hamptons had breached the contract.

It was the second lawsuit that hurt them, though. The man who fell off his ladder sued the Hamptons for $4 million. He had hurt his spine and it was believed he wouldn't be able to go back to work for some time. It was then that the Hamptons discovered that Frank didn't have insurance or any assets.

The Hamptons' lawyer asked them for the contract and the Hamptons realized that they had never received the contract that Frank was supposed to write up.

Mr. Nostrami turned out to be a professional. He wrote the Hamptons a letter in which he enclosed photocopies of his telephone logs which showed when the Hamptons had called and why. It also showed when he called the Hamptons. In fact, twice he had called to ask if he could come by and the Hamptons had declined his offer. His contract, which they had signed, clearly stated that oversight was beyond the scope of his design contract and that he held no responsibility for oversight, fit, and finish unless he was brought to the site once a week. The Hamptons didn't remember reading that part, but their signature was at the bottom of the contract.

The Hamptons called in Prime Construction to look at their kitchen again to see what it would cost to fix up Frank's work. The man from Prime spent ten minutes looking around at the space and reached the conclusion that even though demolishing this kitchen was slightly harder than demolishing their original Tudor kitchen, he would overlook that and he could probably save all but two cabinets. Otherwise, his bid would be the exact same as last time. Demolish one kitchen and start from scratch.

Two days later, the city building inspector came out to reinspect the work according to a date Frank had set a month earlier. The inspector asked for the names of Frank's plumber and electrician. When he found out they weren't licensed, he inspected the work himself and found out that Frank had somehow tapped into an electric line that wasn't even fused—a short circuit would just keep arcing until the whole house had burned down. As for the plumbing Frank had not only hooked up the vent to the waste line but had failed to pitch it.

Under normal circumstances, these would have been serious violations and the inspector would have written up the plumber and electrician for the violations. But in this case, because the job had been started without a building permit, and they had hired unlicensed contractors (Larry Hampton had also tried to pay him off with a fifty-dollar bill), the building inspector revoked the Certificate of Occupancy for the house until the work in the kitchen was corrected. The sheriff had to be called in to evict the Hamptons.

2

Money Problems

I magine that you had $20,000 to spend in two months. You probably wouldn't keep close tabs on the money, figuring so much of it couldn't go that fast. You'd probably check the balance after a month or so, but in the meantime you'd just spend it without thinking about it. You probably wouldn't worry about the price of small purchases too much. Compared to the $20,000, a $200 watch wouldn't matter too much.

Say, for instance, your renovation costs $60,000. Your contractor has asked for a $20,000 down payment.

From now on, the contractor finishes work and you pay him one-third less than the value of that work. For example, the first $10,000 of work would net him $7,000 (the $3,000 makes up for that original down payment). At the beginning, the contractor is still ahead on money, but as the job progresses, he'll have less and less money left over in his pocket because he's having to do more work than he's being paid for. By the end of the job, you should hold at least 10 percent of the money or in this case $6,000. That should protect you; but what if he spent some of that first $20,000 on things other than your project. Perhaps he wasted some money, paid a plumber for another job, and paid the IRS what he owed them. Say he spent $10,000 out of the original $20,000. Toward the end of the job and before the final payment, the owner is holding 10 percent, or $6,000, until the contractor has completed the entire job. With the money the contractor spent at the beginning, he'll be short $16,000 of this $60,000 job. This means the contractor will run short of cash and subcontractors will hold up deliveries until they get paid, expensive hardware may not be bought, and even the labor force may suddenly dwindle.

The contractor can't go to the owners and ask for an advance of the money he's owed, because the owner is going to hold on to that to make sure everything is finally completed.

So the contractor will either hold all his debtors off or, more likely, get another job. Then he can use the next job's down payment to finish this job. The problem for you is that suddenly the contractor and his labor force leave your job right at the most crucial time because he wants to make a good first impression on his new clients.

The end of a job is also when the contractor's ability for self-delusion can take over. He may look in the bank and see $300 and decide that's all the work he has left. He'll say, "Oh, three more days of Dave," one of the contractor's lowest-paid employees, "and we'll have the job finished right on schedule." Three more days of Dave is, incidentally, $192.

Unfortunately, the contractor is underestimating the amount of work left, and what's really needed is three more days of Dave, Brian, and Jay (the contractor's other carpenters). Ignoring this, the contractor will go to Dave and give him the list of all the work that has to be done. Dave, being the lowest-paid employee, will agree to do all this work not knowing that it will be impossible to finish. Dave will fail.

The job won't be finished on time. In trying to finish everything,

Dave will do some things very sloppily, and now there's even more work to be done to correct Dave's mistakes.

Because many contractors don't do a thorough job accounting until the end of the job when they look to see how much money is left, it isn't until then that panic sets in. First, they'll look for either a missed payment, a bounced check, or an employee theft. When they don't find anything, the contractor will realize that the reason they didn't make any money was that they did extra work without billing for it.

So the contractor and the employees walk around the site and remember all the extra things they did and a bill will be presented to the client and the architect. Remember that the client has been living a fantasy that the contractor is a benevolent soul. A bill for thousands of dollars of extras will come as a very unpleasant shock. If they had known the cost, they never would have made the changes in the first place. The statement has finally come for what the contractor made seem like a credit card without a bill.

Endemic to beautiful jobs with forward-thinking clients and architects are extras caused by good design. If clients want an interesting design, architects achieve it by making it unique to the client. Oftentimes these unique designs haven't been tried before so it's nearly impossible to design them perfectly the first time. Mistakes will be made, and the more unique the design, the more chance of mistake. By the end of the job, the cost of these mistakes will start to become apparent. Custom window shutters won't work as planned; honed marble wainscoting in a bathroom will need a custom-milled marble cap to "finish" it; the hidden duct system just doesn't deliver enough air.

As flawed details appear, many architects attempt to get the contractor to pay for fixing them, even if the problem originated in design. They don't like to ask the clients to pay for them, so they hope that the contractor will pony up, the contention being that the contractor should have noticed the problem in the design and that these problems were certainly not the client's fault.

Problems because of unique design *are* the client's fault, but in a positive way. The client wanted a one-of-a-kind design, and such a design will have mistakes because it hasn't been tried before. If architects are afraid of losing their professional standing because of mistakes in the design of custom elements, and contractors aren't paid for fixing these mistakes, everyone will stop building interesting things.

The end of a project can be very expensive. It is the many little things that were forgotten or overlooked or put off through the construction period that makes finishing a renovation job so costly—in both time and money. This final list made by architect and owner is called the punchlist. Every one of those little things was left undone for a reason. The reason the switch cover was never mounted on the mirror in the bathroom was that the hole through the mirror wasn't big enough to put the screws through. (This was the first job I was ever asked to do in New York City. I was offered $50 to put on a light switch cover. I arrived at a very expensive apartment, was ushered into the bathroom, took out my screwdriver, and discovered the hole in the mirror wasn't cut big enough—the mirror covered the screw holes. At the time, I was a little smarter than I am now so I called the general contractor and told him the problem. He came over and worked diligently to enlarge the hole. With the last stroke of his glass cutter, he shattered the mirror.)

Imagine a whole list of little problems that can only be solved if another list of problems is solved first. Tradesmen (carpenters, electricians, plumbers) will usually finish whatever they are working on; but if there are difficult problems they can't solve, they leave it unfinished.

All these little problems and their side problems will end up costing money to rectify, but contractors don't usually have money set aside to pay for them. Many contractors think that there shouldn't be any punchlist if they did a good job, but there are problems on every sort of construction job and contractors must learn to budget for them.

3

Solutions to Money Problems

M any of the money problems commonly experienced at the end of the job will have been avoided by your earlier actions. You'll avoid the extras that are announced at the end of the job by insisting on change orders as they come up. That also means you knew you would be billed for extras and have therefore tried to avoid making many changes.

You've solved the problem of the contractor running out of money by not paying him a big down payment. He'll balk at 15 percent down, but if you stick with it, his supply of money will be limited from the start so that at the end of the job he'll have money in the bank to finish the project properly.

You can't force your contractor to keep account of his money, but choosing a contractor who is fiscally responsible is easy. You should have asked in your reference calls whether the contractor handled money well and if he put in for last-minute extras.

Always insist that the contractor make a profit on your job while delivering a beautiful project. Work with him to do that. If you sense that he's losing money, see if you can help him find out why. It can only help your job. If you notice that the men stop working when the contractor leaves, let him know. If you notice that he spends a lot of time chatting, let him know. If you notice he leaves everything to the last minute, let him know. It might be uncomfortable to do this, but if the contractor realizes he's not going to make money, you'll end up getting bad quality or expensive extras.

Final extras are things that resolve problems that were never solved or that only become obvious once everything else is finished. (Now that everything looks so good, the radiators need to be dip-stripped and repainted.) There will be items from earlier in the job that will have been forgotten until now as well, and there will be items that are caused by mistakes in the design of custom elements.

The final negotiation for these extras is delicate, since you want to end the job on a positive note. This desire for a mutually advantageous final outcome is essential for a continued good relationship. Contractors and architects need ongoing recommendations; owners need ongoing warrantee and service. If the contractor did a good job of identifying problem areas during the design and bidding process and came up with solutions that you and your architect agreed to, the extras on the job should be low. In this case, you'll probably have money within your budget to pay many of these extras. Remember, extras typically add up to under 15 percent of the job. However, if you've spent your contingency funds, these final extras will be difficult to pay and will involve more negotiation. Treat these extras as a problem that everyone is searching for a solution to.

At the end of this negotiation, I recommend that everyone throw in something for free. The contractor may throw in a final questionable extra for free, the owner may throw in a few extra hundred dollars, the architect may take pictures and distribute copies. The items don't have to be large; it's the thought that counts and the mutual appreciation of a job well done.

4

Time
Problems

There is a paradox that sometimes develops toward the end of a construction project. As people become more and more agitated about not finishing, they become more and more resistant to finishing.

This is because architecture, by its nature, is a compromised artistic endeavor. Artists set aside their paintings because they're not right. Poems can be rewritten for years if not abandoned altogether. But very rarely does a piece of architecture get abandoned. It's simply too expensive and too needed. Still, few pieces of architecture will ever be built perfectly because existing conditions, available materials, budget, and available skill will compromise the project.

As a result, clients, architects, and contractors who are expecting total perfection in architecture will always be dissatisfied with the project and resistant to finishing.

As the project nears completion and our perfectionists see the flaws, they will try vainly to perfect all of them. There's a story of the most beautiful woman in the world whose only imperfection was a mole. Her husband was driven crazy by it and finally had it removed. The young woman immediately died.

I recently told this story to one of my most fanatical clients. We have been working on her apartment for four years, and we are nearly completed as of this writing. She decided to have her oak floors stained a dark color. I personally don't like stain because it is impossible, especially on a floor, to be completely consistent in its application. The amount of stain applied, the length of time it sits, the amount that's wiped off, the consistency of the wood—everything must be exactly the same for an even finish. It is not possible to achieve.

To make matters worse, she had a grand piano in the middle of the room, which meant either leaving the piano where it was and staining around it *or* moving the piano, staining one side of the room, then moving the piano again and staining the other side. Although the resulting line of stain would theoretically vanish because the two staining operations were completely identical, I felt it was more prudent to stain the whole living room at once with the piano in place. Better to accept the certain imperfection of the three white spots under the piano wheels than one big line across the middle of the living room. (The rooms were designed around this piano and it would never be moved.)

The thought of these white spots was unacceptable to my client. So we stained and polyurethaned half the floor at a time. Though she had approved the method of staining, after the floors were completed, she found some flaws in the staining including the line between the two halves of the floor.

She then insisted that the floors be redone. We sanded off all the stain, restained, and watched as the stain came out ten times worse. Two days later we sanded that stain off again and came up with a floor that was no better than our first effort. Everyone felt horrible by the end.

·   ·   ·

Finishing is difficult for the contractor because he is constantly underestimating the time required to finish. Part of this is his unwillingness to accept the imperfections of framing and foundation. Because a wall is slightly out of plumb, the door won't sit properly in the jamb. Rather than accepting that and dealing with it in some thorough but ultimately time-effective way, like cutting a hole in the Sheetrock, taking out the screws, and moving the whole wall over, many contractors will figure that five minutes of fiddling with the hinges will solve the problem. That method usually doesn't work; but there's a good possibility that the contractor will waste a lot of time trying to make it work.

Earlier in this book, I mentioned Robert Pirsig's *Zen and the Art of Motorcycle Maintenance* and his Gumption Traps. If you recall, I compared his frustration and subsequent inaction after rounding off a nut to losing phone numbers and losing specifications. Now we've got the actual rounded-off nuts: the shower valve that will take two weeks to get the replacement stem for; the door opening that turns out to be too narrow for anything but a custom-made door; the light fixture that has been sitting around for four weeks in an undamaged box turns out to be broken. All of these things stop progress.

Plus, the contractor has had to start working on that next job, splitting his time and delegating tricky bits of work to carpenters who screw things up even more.

It's difficult, too, for the contractor to commit himself to completely finishing the punchlist because he knows how long it will take and that it will require his best men. Instead, he will postpone fixing the final details, even though it holds up his final payment, because he doesn't want to see how little money he has left.

Like the contractor, the architect may also be working on her next job, so she'll be slow to make decisions or neglectful in ordering the finishing touches.

The owners can also be resistant to finishing. Frequently, it is the first time in their lives that they have had servants, someone to put up a shelf, fix the refrigerator, take a message. Particularly if the owner is lonely, there is a reluctance to letting a nice contractor leave.

Suddenly, there is a stream of ongoing changes and rejection of work. A fanatical search for perfection can set in with the fear of the contractor leaving with things less than finished. One client complained that paint was smeared on the underside of a step. Fair enough until I remembered that this was a one-floor apartment. The step was to the balcony and the only way the smear was visible was to lie down with your cheek on the floor. I asked him whether that would be a common position for him.

Many clients worry that they've been too relaxed and believe that now is the time to crack down. If they were lax from the beginning, it's too late now. They might get some small improvements but it will usually cause big delays.

5

Solutions to
Time Problems

Now is the time to help push the project to completion by realistically budgeting the time left for the contractor and reminding him of what he's forgotten. A good original cost breakdown will be a fine friend now. By paging through all the items in the contractor's breakdown, you will discover what he has forgotten up to now.

List individual items that still need to be done. The more the contractor has specifics in front of him, the more able he will be to correctly budget and estimate his time. Don't let him think that everything is under control if it's not.

Jobs that don't finish on schedule will not make the contractor money because his overhead and cleanup costs add to the cost of the job each day he's late. Be positive but clear that the deadline that the contractor agreed to in the beginning is still what you expect, allowing for specific changes caused by change orders. At each weekly meeting, ask the contractor to spell out his plans to finish the job within the allotted time.

On the other hand, if your job is truly behind schedule despite everyone's efforts, don't force the contractor to an unrealistic deadline that will cause more mistakes. Use common sense: An extension of a week or two might be just what's needed to get your job finished beautifully. Don't let the contractor think that this is easy for you, or that another extension is possible, especially if the contractor has started another job, which he likely has.

As the job winds down, ask the contractor to walk the job and make up a preliminary punchlist of unfinished or imperfect items. Clients shouldn't make their own list themselves for two reasons: (1) they'll be complaining about things the contractor is going to fix anyway, and (2) a client's early list will focus more on gross items (door to kitchen not installed) rather than individual, specific quality problems (door to kitchen rubs against frame).

Better to let the contractor find fault with his own work. It will then become a matter of pride to finish your job well and show you how attentive to detail he is. Then, when he's finished, you'll find what he's missed (see preceding chapter).

Keep up the idea that your job is a trophy: bring by friends who are considering their own renovations; try to get your local newspaper to take pictures and do a story; let the contractor know you've started a recommendation letter and show him a draft. All of these things will keep his energy up as he faces the Gumption Traps that finishing any construction project generates.

Never relent in your pressure toward completion. Never say "whenever" or "whatever." The contractor is tired now, you must not let him off the hook. Though it will be tough on him, later he'll be happy that he finished on time and made a profit. Planning for a housewarming party shortly after the completion date can also give everyone an excuse to work faster.

At the end of a job it's possible that you'll be dealing not with the contractor himself, but with a job foreman. In this case, you have to extend your efforts to both contractor and foreman, and if you can see they're not doing what they should be doing, let both of them know.

Don't waste everyone's time by making judgments on items that haven't been finished. The only thing that looks good in progress is beige on beige. If you've made more interesting choices, you have to see the job in its completed stage down to drapes on the windows and flowers on the table. Refer to the colored, perspective drawings. I have seen so many interesting schemes changed into blandness by clients who got skittish about strong choices. Often, the clients never saw a proper colored sketch of the project. Instead they were asked to look at a sample board of paint chips and fabric swatches—a poor way to imagine a finished room.

Reserve judgment on design issues until the project is completed. Then, if the color of the kitchen really doesn't work, you can call the painter back to repaint. Accent colors can change the entire look of a color, and until these accent colors are in place, it is difficult to judge the wall color.

Finally, accept that construction isn't perfect. Some compromise will let you get the things that are truly important while allowing the project as a whole to go forward.

6

Power
Problems

Toward the end of construction, contractor, owner, and architect realize that their ongoing relationship will soon be over. A fear can set in that someone might now try to take advantage of another. The contractor might take the substantial amount of money he's already been paid and abandon the job; the owner could wait until the project is completed and then not pay the contractor or the architect the balance of his or her bill; or the future project the architect has been dangling in front of the contractor like a carrot could suddenly be yanked away.

In an ongoing relationship these fears are unfounded, but in construction, where owners and contractors won't likely need to do business again, there isn't much inclination toward an ongoing friendship.

There may also be some feelings in the owners that they've been held over a barrel; that they were forced to put down a large initial deposit; that they've had to pay for unfair extras just to keep the job going. There may be a desire for revenge now.

The clients ultimate power is to pay the final bills and to recommend the contractor and architect.

An unhappy owner is worth nothing to an architect and contractor who are constantly looking for new jobs. A happy customer can lead to two more jobs, which can lead to four more jobs, which can lead to sixteen. One very happy customer can make a contractor's business. An unhappy customer will do nothing and the contractor has spent three months of his life for the little money he has at the end of a project.

Let your happiness and unhappiness be known. A contractor can argue that a joint is good or a finish is fine, but he can't argue with your unhappiness.

The contractor's power lies in his ability to finish the job well, to go the extra mile and to warrantee the job. His satisfaction with the final resolution of the job is important to the owner as well. If the contractor feels he's been taken advantage of, or has lost money on the job, he'll resist returning to fix things cheerfully and quickly later on.

Curiously, the contractor also has the power to recommend architects. I'm often approached first for jobs because people have heard good things from former clients and are hoping to do the work without the aid of an architect. In these cases I usually advise the client to hire an architect and I always recommend my favorites.

Architects also seem to forget that contractors won't always say yes to working for them. Architects are constantly crossed off contractors' lists for sins of sloppy design, bad paperwork, and general unfairness.

The architect has the power to advise the client regarding the final payment to the contractor, and to recommend the contractor to other clients.

The architect also has the power to take the raw finished space and help the owners to make it into a home. I've built many beautiful spaces, but some of them still look completely sterile and empty. This is because the owner has failed to work with the architect to the end of the project. Other owners have kept on the architect or have hired a separate designer to help with the furniture buying, drape selection, and decorating that help the project reach its true potential.

The architect also has the de facto role of "neutral" mediator between client and contractor, although the architect is obviously not neutral, since she's the owner's representative. The architect is paid by the client, wants the client to recommend her to friends, and is bound contractually to defend the client's rights. Yet the architect is called in to mediate disputes between the contractor, client, and architect.

Even the standard AIA contract establishes the architect as the usual decider of disputes. In most cases the architect is fair and the contractor and the client will be happy with the mediation. However, there are times the architect will not be totally fair, particularly if the architect or owner is at fault. But even if the architect is completely neutral, there is always the risk that the client will view this as disloyalty.

Because the client is ignorant of the business of construction, anything that feels unfair will be perceived as collusion between the architect and contractor. This forces the architect to be unfair to the contractor just so that the client doesn't feel slighted.

7

Solutions to Power Problems

I t is essential to remember the ongoing nature of the three-way relationship between the owner, contractor, and architect. In order to set the contractor at ease regarding final payment, owners should remind the contractor that they will need him in the future for warrantee repairs and future work and as someone they can refer friends to.

By the same token, you should let the architect know you will continue to need her services as you furnish your project. If this is inappropriate (say it's a kitchen and all appliances and fixtures have already been decided), then arranging a dinner for the architect and some friends is a great way to keep the architect pulling through to the end. Nothing makes an architect more particular about refining the details of her work than imagining sitting with potential clients three months from now in a space she's designed.

The contractor likewise must reassure the clients that he wants them to be happy with the result. The contractor should ask to take photos of the job and request a letter of recommendation. It will put the architect at ease to hear the contractor asking what other jobs he might bid on.

It's proven that forcing a smile has many of the same neurological benefits as a real smile. Simple expressions of friendship can influence a relationship in a positive way, even if they are not entirely heartfelt. Architects who dangle future jobs for contractors they haven't enjoyed working with may find the contractor's work improving to the point that he earns the right to bid.

Forcing yourself to work cooperatively brings about changes that lead to natural cooperation. Some architects and contractors may not live up to their reputation, but unless your job is a large-scale disaster, or there are big problems right off the bat, I recommend against firing either one of them. Instead, I advocate a careful initial screening process, then a full effort toward working as a team.

As the project's end nears, let the contractor and architect know how much you look forward to seeing the finished project and writing the final check. Make it clear exactly what has to be done to achieve this completion.

After the project ends, and you make the final payment, you will have warrantee repairs or adjustments. Think of these as the contractor taking care of his work of art. If you act as though you assume the contractor wants to keep the job perfect, he will likely act that way, too. Most contractors will stand behind their work and you can help by framing the repairs positively. If the pipes are banging, don't call and say, "Fred, these pipes are driving me crazy. I'm so angry at the plumber. I knew this was going to happen. You need to fix this now." Instead, try, "Fred, you're going to hate to hear this but those pipes are banging again. You worked so hard last time. What do you think you can do to get them to stop?" No reasonable contractor would hesitate to take care of your pipes if you frame the problem in such a manner.

If there are disputes, the contractor, architect, and client should meet together to work them out. If this doesn't work, use a mediator.

Qualified mediators are becoming more available and can be found through your local American Arbitration Association, through the Better Business Bureau, or through the American Renovation Association, which will soon offer a telephone mediation service. There's a full overview of dispute resolution in the appendices.

Now would be a good time to read the Dispute Resolution section of the appendix.

8

Management Problems

Trying to pull together all the loose ends of a full-size project is difficult. If you've hired a good contractor, he is using his full experience, talent, and energy to bring everything to a close. But despite this, he is probably making some mistakes.

Contractors, like the rest of us, are not able to think critically and work physically at the same time. At the end of a job, you may find your contractor working very hard but perhaps not planning through to completion very well.

At the same time, potential clients are approaching the contractor for their renovations. He will bid new projects and give these clients a start date for construction. When your project runs over schedule, he will give the new client a later date. This client will then threaten to hire someone else. To save the new job, your contractor may try to be in two places at one time, thinking that your job is at the final stage. (We've proved, though, that the end of a project takes the most attention.)

After part of the tools and manpower have moved onto the next job, the client may have a few more bits of work to be done. A client once asked me to add a step out onto his rooftop terrace. It was at the end of the project and this one little board on two legs required at least thirty tools to build. The final stage of any project is often filled with these kinds of "odds and ends" projects that can drag on as tools and men are ferried back and forth.

This whole situation reaches its zenith when the contractor sends his assistant to finish your punchlist and the assistant isn't sure of what the problem is and can't find the proper tool to fix it.

The architect may have moved on to other projects as well, so she may not have the time to monitor the contractor's work either.

No wonder owners often get angry at this stage. The architect, contractor, and crew are gone, leaving in their place one dazed assistant with no tools.

9

Solutions to Management Problems

A few pages ago I recommended a diplomatic way of calling back a contractor to fix something. Now I'm going to suggest a stronger means of keeping your project well managed through its completion.

Since it is likely that your contractor will have the opportunity to move on to his next project before he finishes yours, you must devise a strategy to make sure he finishes your project on time. Remember, it is in the best interests of the contractor and the architect to finish well: Your positive recommendation will be a positive asset to them in the future. To this end:

- Ask the contractor casually what other projects he is lining up and how he plans to fit those around finishing your job. Find out when it starts, how big it is, and who might be pulled off your job.

- Don't accept the myth that your job will be easy to finish and that your contractor has time to fit in another job.

- Ask the contractor to make a list of the work he has to do to satisfy himself, then set aside a formal meeting to go through it with him and the architect.

As you go through the contractor's list and see items like "Install door in bathroom," ask why the door hasn't been installed yet. You may find out that the door was framed incorrectly and that it will be difficult to set right. As you go down the list, use your judgment to point out items that will be difficult to finish. The idea here is that you want to reinforce how much work there is yet to be done.

Once you've seen how much work there is to do, tell the contractor how concerned you are about everything getting finished. Let the contractor know that you've been telling friends about how things have been on schedule and how pleased you've been with his work so far. But now you are concerned.

Do this toward the last third of the job. If it's a three-month job, use this strategy at two months. Follow this plan and you should keep your architect and contractor working to finish your renovation.

If you see that work on your job is slowing to a snail's pace, complain immediately. If you see that the subcontractors aren't finishing their part of the work, complain to your contractor. Subcontractors think they are invisible, but it has been my experience that if a client complains about a subcontractor, his work improves immediately.

Finally, keep everyone focused on the shared goal: a beautiful renovation, on time and on budget.

10

Quality Problems

Even though you can't actually see the quality of your renovation until the end of construction, the quality has been decided in the previous stages of the project.

If you've done the work in this book, you have a good design that was reviewed by a contractor. You've set quality standards at the beginning of construction and you posted what you'll be looking for at the end of the project. You've introduced yourself to the subcontractors and you have worked fairly with your contractor and architect at weekly meetings.

If you have problems now, you've missed something and it may be too late to change it.

Quality at the end of construction depends on the quality of the underlying structure. It's hard to hang a cabinet properly on a crooked wall. Sheetrock that wasn't taped by professionals will look terrible once you paint it. A light fixture that's out of center will make the whole dining room look "off."

These are difficult things to change.

At the end of the project, there are also problems caused by a desire by tradesmen to get out of the job. It takes a minute to attach a cabinet door using adjustable hinges. It can take another five minutes to get the hinge adjusted perfectly. The carpenter may have the twenty minutes to put on all the cabinet doors, but not the hour and a half necessary to adjust them right. The final paint touch-ups will find painters applying paint and dripping all over your hardware because they don't want to take the time to protect. Plumbers may also be pushed to finish and install sinks without paying attention to how square they are to the countertop.

These problems are correctable and their uncorrected presence can ruin the final look of your renovation.

11

Solutions to Quality Problems

Once your contractor has finished the job, walk through the renovation with the architect. Slowly and carefully inspect the finished product. This should take place in the daytime when you have plenty of natural light. Use the quality checklist from the "Beginning Construction" section. The purpose of this list is not to get a *perfect* job (otherwise you'll be lying down on the floor looking for paint smears on the underside of steps), but to perfect the job in terms of your utility and aesthetics. Are things centered and level to the eye; do the cabinets all work well; do things look finished to you?

Once this list is handed over to the contractor, there may be things that are unreasonable to fix. Bumps in linoleum may be air bubbles that can be worked out, or they could be a lump of glue or some other debris, in which case the whole floor would have to be torn out. Forcing a contractor to rip something out and redo it at this stage of the game will probably create a lot of hard feelings, inconvenience, and plain old trouble. It may be easier to negotiate a monetary settlement for things that are truly unacceptable but too difficult to repair.

With luck, though, your contractor will be able to fix most of the problems and may even enjoy the opportunity to make things perfect.

All homeowners should have a well-stocked toolbox of their own. If you don't have one, this is a great time and excuse to get one. You should also ask the contractor for any leftover hardware (screws, nuts, drawer pulls, hooks, etc.) that he did not use in your project. Keep these in a safe place in case you need to use them.

It's common that a contractor will drop in to take care of warrantee problems when he's "in the neighborhood." Typically, the contractor won't have all his tools with him and often he'll use yours. Any hardware that you have will also come in handy during the warrantee year. Having your own tools allows the contractor to stop by when he's not prepared to do a service call.

Finally, keep this in mind as you look at your finished renovation: What is now a glaring error in an empty room will soon be hidden by furniture, magazines, and children. Work to get a beautiful project but balance it with the need to have it finish on time and on budget.

Construction is a human process. Flaws are just a reminder that people have done this work.

12

The Finleys— the Completion of a Dream Kitchen

Michelle picked up the phone at her battered desk in the humanities department. "Hello."

"Hi, Michelle, it's Chris. I just talked to Giovanni about bidding another project I'm doing and he said he has another project he's probably going to start in a couple of days."

"That's terrible."

"I know, that's why I called. I asked him if he was going to stay on your job and he said he'd be there as much as he could, but I'm worried because they're putting in the cabinets this week and there are doors to hang and countertops to install. I really need Giovanni there. I like his son, but I know he won't be able to do as good a job and I have such high hopes right now."

"Should I talk to him or should you?"

"I can probably be more of a heavy than you."

"I think," Michelle said, "my happiness is as valuable to Mr.

DeTomaso as the money. Right now it's hard to tell what anything will look like. I know the walls are plumb, I know the ceiling light box is in the right place, I know the walls are smooth. But otherwise, I can't tell if it's a nice kitchen or not. I'm afraid when he leaves, we could end up with a bad job and then we've all lost."

"So, *you* call him."

"Giovanni DeTomaso." It was his standard phone greeting.

"Michelle Finley. How are you, Giovanni?"

"Afraid you're going to complain about my next job. You call to say, 'Don't work for anyone but me, Giovanni, I pay you the rest of my life.' "

"Not quite, and exaggerating isn't necessary, but I'm very concerned about what I've heard and I wanted to ask you what's going on. This job has been going well so far but I know that I need your best carpenter right now, and that person is you. As much as I respect and like the people who work for you, I know that you are the one who should be there for all of this finish carpentry. I think our kitchen could be really special and I want you to prosper from that as well. So far we've brought two sets of friends to the job site and they were very impressed by what you've done. I don't want to see this opportunity slip by us all and have this be just another job."

"Mrs. Finley, you speak very nicely, and I agree with you. We want this to be a beautiful job. For me, it's very difficult. I must balance doing for you a perfect job now, and for me having a paycheck next month. This other job starts next week and if I don't do it, someone else will."

"Why is that?"

"The lady tells me so."

"Who is as good as Giovanni DeTomaso? No one. Let me speak to her. If she has any brains she waits, and if she waits for you, then I bet you would return her the favor at the end of her job."

"No, I cannot let you do that, Mrs. Finley."

"Giovanni, have we been very good clients?"

"Yes."

"We've paid on time, we bring friends by, we don't change our minds?"

"Yes."

"And you, too, have been top-quality, clean, neat, dependable, excellent quality, clear payment requests, fair extra pricing, you return calls. Let me speak to this other client. It can't hurt you, but without it I can see we will have a very hard time between us and I don't want that."

"My son is very good."

"Yes, but I did not hire your son. Can your son start this other lady's house?"

There was silence.

"Then let me speak to her. What is her name?"

"She is Mrs. Randleman."

"I will sing your high praises."

"But I can't wait until the very end of the job."

"Why, is the punchlist the easiest part? I've always heard it's the most difficult part of the job, the most likely place for the contractor to lose money."

"You read this?"

"Yes. Is it true?"

There was silence again on DeTomaso's line. "I never have one client speak to another."

"But, Giovanni, the best of all possible worlds is that you finish my job on time as promised, in perfect shape, I recommend you to all my friends, and you start Mrs. Randleman's job as soon as mine is finished. Wouldn't that be best?"

Giovanni DeTomaso sighed. "I call her, Mrs. Finley."

"Are you sure?"

"I think you're crazy but I try my best."

"Thank you, Giovanni. When are the cabinets going in?"

"Next Tuesday."

.   .   .

Mrs. Randleman was not happy to be pushed back, but
DeTomaso did his best to make Mrs. Finley's points. In the end, it
was DeTomaso's promise that he would do the same for her at the end
of her job; and that he would start in three weeks, the intended
completion date for the Finleys' renovation.

Construction seemed to speed up even more in anticipation of
actually completing the job on time. For the meeting three weeks
before completion, Chris Layner asked DeTomaso to write up a complete list of everything that was still to be done and its scheduling so
that the Finleys and she would be able to provide him with everything
he needed to finish on time. DeTomaso did not want to do this list
because he was so busy installing cabinets, but Chris made it clear
that it was nonnegotiable. This was her "three-week list" and it was
essential to finishing the job on time successfully without anything
being forgotten and causing a delay.

The lower cabinets were installed, leveled, and screwed together
for the meeting, and the templates for the countertops were laid out.
Everything looked beautiful. The Finleys, Giovanni, and Chris
Layner were standing around the island, their papers on the Masonite
template.

"So here is the list Ms. Layner made me do," Giovanni said. "She
is crazy making me do this list but I find that it's quite interesting
despite her. I realize we still don't know the color of the ceiling. I
notice you haven't given me the light fixture choice yet and I notice I
have no sink."

Chris Layner spoke. "This is very good, Giovanni. I notice,
though, that you don't have any time set aside for doing the punchlist
we give you at the end."

"I would like to get your final punchlist at the beginning of the
final week."

"Giovanni, at the beginning of your final week, I would like you
to go around with me so we can make a 'pre' punchlist. These are all
the things that you are planning to do but haven't done yet. I'll be

with you so that if there are problems with those things, maybe we can work them out.

"Then," Chris continued, "when you are finished, I will go through the job with the Finleys and we'll make one final punchlist. My guess is that there will only be a few things on that list. You will fix those things and that is that."

"That is fine, but realistically, Ms. Layner, when do I have the time to do those things? I'm a little behind right now. It will be everything I can do to finish my list by the time I start Mrs. Randleman's job."

"Do you think you can be completed with everything on your list by the eighteenth?"

"Yes."

"So, finish by the sixteenth and—"

"No, the eighteenth." DeTomaso was tired of being managed.

"I'm sorry," Chris said. "You're being reasonable and I'm pushing you. What do you think we should do?"

"Give me to the eighteenth, I do a beautiful job. Then the Finleys start using the kitchen, see how things are, maybe they notice a few more things, maybe they dent a wall moving in. Two weeks from now I take a day off from Mrs. Randleman and I personally fix everything up."

Tom smiled immediately. "Sold. Very good. That's great. I didn't know how we were going to get out of that."

"What if there's a big list?" Chris asked politely.

"There won't be a big list," Giovanni assured.

"If you're so sure, would you mind agreeing that if the list is very large—the kind of things that would prevent the Finleys from moving in—you would stay and fix those things even if it meant starting your other job late? I'm sure that won't be necessary, but if you would agree to that proviso, I'd highly recommend the Finleys accept your plan."

Chris caught the embarrassed look on Tom's face for his premature agreement.

"I just need to make sure everything is clear, Tom. Do we have a deal, Mr. DeTomaso?"

Giovanni nodded. "Fine. You wear me down."

"I don't mean to, Mr. DeTomaso. I think you're great and I want to make sure the Finleys get their money's worth." Chris smiled then and added, "You are, after all, the best and most expensive contractor around."

Giovanni smiled back. "Very well."

"Here," Chris said, "let me write this up."

And Chris wrote it up and they all signed it, though they felt very foolish about it.

It was late at night and Tom was just going upstairs when he saw Michelle standing in the kitchen, color fan deck in hand, looking back and forth at the wall.

"Anything I can help you with?"

Michelle came out of her trance. "Do you think this color is right?"

"Who can tell?"

"No, I mean, isn't it too green? I think something lighter would be better. It makes everything seem dark."

Tom looked at her, relieved that for once it was Michelle who was being an ass, worrying about an unfinished detail. His tone was extra patronizing. "Honey, is everything else in the kitchen yet? Didn't we look at a watercolor sketch of the whole kitchen with all the colors?"

"But that was a drawing. This is too green."

"But the reds aren't up yet, right? The reds are going to contrast with the greens and balance them. That's what Chris said."

"But I don't like this."

Tom realized Michelle was serious. Then his face lit up. "Wait, I think we still have that picture. Chris warned us that we might have second thoughts before everything was together and that we should wait until we saw the big picture."

Tom rummaged through their job file and then found the drawing on the dining table, which was currently in the living room. "Here it is. What do you think now?"

Michelle looked at the picture, then looked at the walls. Back at the picture. Back at the walls. "Let's go to bed. I'll wait until they're done and then blame you."

"Thank you, honey," Tom said as he turned out the kitchen light and led her upstairs.

DeTomaso finished the kitchen exactly on time and it looked terrific. The doors in the cabinets were aligned, the seams in the countertops were hardly visible. The dishwasher worked perfectly on the first try (because DeTomaso had run it first and found it leaked at a gasket and called in the appliance company immediately to repair it). The design of the kitchen was also very pleasing and everything looked more or less as they had pictured it. The green was strong, but the red trim balanced it just as it did in the perspective drawing. DeTomaso had done his walk-through with Chris, made a long list of problems which Chris resolved, so the final list, as anticipated, was short. There was some paint on the door hinges that DeTomaso had missed. The dishwasher wasn't screwed in properly and it was a little crooked in the opening. (Later it was discovered that it had been installed perfectly but when the unit was repaired, the repairman took out the screws and didn't replace them correctly.) One of the dimmers hummed and the windows were dirty. That was about all. While they waited for these final details to be worked out, Giovanni sent them the final bill.

Chris Layner saw the blinking lights on her answering machine and turned it on with her usual mix of anticipation and dread. "Hello, Chris? This is Tom Finley. Please give me a call. We just received the final bill from DeTomaso and he has in here six hundred bucks for trim pieces for the kitchen. He never told us about that. Every other extra we've approved in advance. He knew he was doing a kitchen. This is ridiculous. What's he trying to get? A tip? Give me a call."

Beep.

"Hello, Ms. Layner. Giovanni DeTomaso. Listen to me. I sent in a final bill to the Finleys and I wanted to tell you before they got it—I had to charge extra for the trim strips for the kitchen. The kitchen didn't come with them and we had to make them in the shop and finish them so that the cabinets would come together in the corners and at the sides. I'm sorry I didn't call you before but we were so busy at first I just wanted to finish the kitchen and I didn't want to go in with all the paperwork and I didn't know how much they cost. I don't know. Maybe you should call me before they get the bill."

Beep.

Chris turned off the machine. She hated things like this. Hated them! Why didn't he just call her before he made all these strips? She had ordered the kitchen cabinets with the strips. They probably hadn't been delivered. The amazing thing, though, was that she hadn't noticed. She would look when she went back, but she hadn't even noticed the difference between the manufactured cabinet doors and what DeTomaso had done.

Now Tom listened to the messages on his answering machine. "Hello, Tom, this is Chris. I got your message. Giovanni called me, too. I think we should all get together and talk this over. I'd like to meet at your earliest convenience. Tomorrow night would be good for me or Friday morning. Thanks."

Tom looked at Michelle. "What are we supposed to talk over? It sounds like they're going to gang up on us. Doesn't Chris make more money the more DeTomaso charges us?"

"Tom, remember what you told me about the color. Wait until we see the whole picture? I know it's six hundred dollars. I'm not excited about paying it but I want to hear his side of the story."

The phone rang. Michelle picked it up. "Hello."

"Yes, Giovanni DeTomaso. Listen, I don't want any bad blood to come between us and I understand from Chris that you're not happy about the extra cabinet pieces. She suggest we get together to talk about it but I know myself too well. Nothing against you but I'm going to get excited and I can't express myself too well and I know that

Chris has to be on your side because she's getting paid by you. Remember the mediator we call up for the hundred dollars who will do a half-hour conference call? I think now's a good time to use him."

Michelle looked at the phone. "Let me talk to Chris and Tom about this and I'll call you back. We can call this man at any time?"

"Business hours."

"Okay, did you give us a brochure or anything on him?"

"I did but I fax it again to Chris."

Michelle hung up the phone and looked at Tom. "Did you follow that? He wants to use the mediator we named in the contract to resolve this."

Tom whined, "Can't we just straighten this out ourselves?"

Michelle shrugged her shoulders. "I have a feeling that DeTomaso feels pretty strongly about the whole thing and I know we do, too. I have a feeling that if we jump into this, it's not going to end well."

Giovanni was sitting in his kitchen, listening to the mediator over the phone.

"So, Mr. DeTomaso, their point is that the kitchen panels had been ordered and that they just didn't arrive. If you had let them know, they would have checked with the store and it wouldn't have ended up costing six hundred dollars."

Giovanni was silent on the phone line for just a moment. Then he said, "The Finleys were responsible for getting everything there."

The mediator asked, "You don't think you had some responsibility in letting them know if it wasn't there?"

The Finleys, too, were sitting at their kitchen table, listening to the phone.

"So, Mr. and Mrs. Finley, Mr. DeTomaso's point is that he was doing the best job he could, getting everything done on time. When the problem came up, he assumed, incorrectly, that the filler strips didn't come with the cabinets. Apparently, according to him, stock cabinets usually don't come with filler strips so he didn't think twice about it. He says that his strips were so expensive because he had to custom-match the wood and the finish on the wood. How do they look?"

"Very good."

"Did you ever get the filler strips?"

"Well, we called the store, they said they were still on order."

"So he couldn't have finished the kitchen had he waited. Would that have been okay with you?"

"Well, he was going on to another job, so it would have been difficult to get him back."

"What was the value of those trim pieces and are they refunding that to you?"

"Two hundred and fifty dollars."

"I don't imagine you have any problem with paying Mr. DeTomaso at least that, right?"

"No," Tom said, "that would be fine."

"Well, what would you think about a premium, since Mr. DeTomaso was able to finish your kitchen on time? And why weren't the pieces with the cabinets when they arrived? Had they been on order long, or had you ordered the cabinets late?"

"Well, we didn't order them as soon as we could have."

"Hmmm. Let me talk to Mr. DeTomaso again."

"Mr. DeTomaso, they tell me the filler pieces are worth about two hundred and fifty dollars. As a beginning, they certainly wouldn't have any problem paying you that, so we are really only three hundred and fifty dollars apart."

"So do we split that?"

"No, not necessarily. The issues that are still remaining are that you didn't let them know so they could have taken action, or at least had a choice in the matter."

"I know. I blew it. If I said six hundred, they would have thought that too much. Then I would have told them it's not possible to get those other pieces for another three weeks. You want to pay me extra to put them in then."

"How much would you have charged to come back to put them in?"

"That's quite a bit of work."

"Well, you had to put them in anyway. You would have put them in later."

"Not so easy. If I put them in later, it would be after the painter was finished. Filler pieces are meant to be very tight so I definitely would have scraped the new paint. Plus, I had to cut the filler pieces. You try it. There's a lot of sawdust. I don't think they would want that in their clean kitchen so I have to measure inside, run outside, make another cut, run back in, see if it fits, run back out, cut again. It's twice the work. I'll be honest with you. The painter maybe charge a hundred twenty-five to touch up. But they use eggshell, and so if you touch it up, there's a funny sheen around the touch-up. So then you have to roll out the whole wall again. So maybe one hundred fifty. For me to bring back my tools and set up again is at least two hundred dollars, and cutting outside and cleaning up a finished kitchen is going to be another two hundred dollars over what I charged them to install the kitchen."

"Mr. DeTomaso, I tape-recorded that part. Would you mind if I played that back to them? Maybe they would have a better understanding of why you did what you did."

"Go ahead. They're very nice people and I apologize for not calling them. It just seemed like the sensible thing to do and I was going crazy trying to finish the job for them."

The Finleys and Mr. DeTomaso came to an amicable agreement. Mr. DeTomaso reduced his price for the confusion he'd caused, but for the most part, now that the Finleys understood what the work had saved them, they were happy to pay what he asked.

Since then, Mr. DeTomaso has returned to adjust a door that had sagged on one of the cabinets, got the icemaker in the refrigerator to work, and installed some coat hooks for free at the same time he was fixing the refrigerator.

The Finleys have recommended him to three sets of friends; one has hired him so far and was thankful to the Finleys for introducing them.

Chris Layner had taken many "before" photographs, and when she coupled those with good "after" shots, she managed to get a photo spread in the design section of the local newspaper. Her business has increased threefold since, and she has kept DeTomaso working steadily in the neighborhood.

Ending Construction Checklist

Money

- Pay according to the pay schedule.
- Insist that work is finished before paying for it (in the final stages).
- Be sure the contractor and architect make a profit on your job.

Time

- Keep the pressure on and a positive attitude.
- Ask the contractor to develop a preliminary punchlist himself.
- Keep your contractor on the job with penalty clauses, future recommendations, and a premium for early completion.
- Maintain good relations with the contractor's job site manager if there is one.
- Schedule a party or other event to hold the contractor to the deadline.
- Reserve judgment on design choices (colors, fabrics) until final completion. Then change elements if you must.
- Work through completion anxiety and put your building project in proper perspective.

Power

- Maintain your public enthusiasm about having a beautiful project, on time and on budget.
- Use your final payment as a carrot to speedy completion.
- Prepare letters of recommendation.
- Use a professional neutral to resolve final disputes over money or other unresolved conflicts.

- Examine the finished product with the architect for its suitability and make adjustments as needed.
- Treat warrantee repairs as something the contractor takes care of out of a sense of pride.

Management

- Tie up the project's loose ends one at a time.
- Use the contractor's punchlist to help him see how much work there is left at three weeks and then one week before completion.
- Don't allow the architect and contractor to shortchange the job at the end and ruin their reputation with you.
- Refuse inferior work quickly.
- Avoid panic by focusing on the mutual goal, a beautiful project on time and on budget.

Quality

- Use your posted quality checklist during walk-throughs and accept nothing less.
- Keep a set of good-quality tools of your own on the job site after the job is finished for the contractor to borrow if he needs to.
- Remember, no job is perfect. Don't drive yourself crazy. Concentrate on what is important.

Conclusion

The work I've suggested here is difficult, and you probably didn't accomplish more than 80 percent of it. But I hope that better understanding the people who are working with you, and what they need, has helped your whole project go better.

I would be very interested to hear how things go, and to hear any suggestions you might have for improving the process of residential construction. You can reach me at:

The American Renovation Association
112 Madison Avenue
New York, NY 10016-7424

Good luck.

Appendices

Materials

Every contractor will have his own advice about materials depending on his particular experience. A nightmare job using a wood edge on Formica countertops may leave one contractor swearing off them while another contractor will use them as his trademark.

The best materials often vary by region. Tile for roofing may work very well in California because of its heat resistance, but it is a poor choice in New England where melting snow and freezing temperatures increase the chance of breakage. Ordering a custom-made marble countertop in New York may be easy because of the many immigrant marble workers who live there, but asking for a Fior di Pesco tub surround in Missoula, Montana, is going to leave most contractors scratching their heads. On the other hand, a solid-surface countertop with a seamless sink will probably be easier to get in Missoula.

Still, I have some opinions about materials, and like everything else in this book, I'm going to make them known. For the most part, I'll try to arrange materials from least expensive to most expensive.

Foundation

The foundation is the underlying support for either a renovation or a new house. There are three main types of foundation: slab, block, and poured concrete.

- A slab foundation is a pad of concrete poured directly on the ground. Using a slab foundation means there'll be no basement—and therefore no room to run plumbing or electric unless you put it in before you pour the concrete. Slab foundations often crack depending on ground, temperature, and water conditions. However, if you can't afford a basement or conditions (such as high groundwater) don't permit one, slab foundations are fast and economical. Plus, you won't have to build a floor; it's already there, though a bit hard. Make sure to watch for a smooth and level slab formed by a single pour.

■ Block foundations are built of concrete blocks or cinder blocks laid up like bricks with mortar in between. Block walls aren't as strong as poured reinforced concrete. The dirt on the other side of the foundation exerts pressure so that block basements can't be built as deep. Not being as strong, block foundations are also more likely to crack with shifting earth (though you can patch this crack with another application of mortar).

Block foundations can be constructed in tight or out-of-the-way locations which might preclude concrete mixer trucks. They are simple to build, requiring only the blocks, mortar, and a mason. Constructed by a professional and swept off when completed (meaning a brush is passed over the block to clean up the mortared joints), the block work can be simply painted and can look quite presentable. They are economical because they don't require carpenters to build forms, cement trucks, and crews of men to oversee the pouring of the cement.

Block work is a good choice for shallow basements or crawl spaces under additions because they don't cause the wear and tear on the site that pouring concrete can cause. Make sure that the walls are straight and plumb with well-finished joints.

■ Poured concrete foundations are made by pouring cement into forms constructed out of wood or metal. The forms are somewhat expensive to erect, and getting the cement to the forms may be difficult depending on your site. Either a truck will have to back up across your property, or they'll have to use a pump truck or cart it by wheelbarrow. All of these can be expensive. When the forms are taken down, it is likely that there will be holes in the face of the cement (from air bubbles), and stone in the mix will show through. Even patched, this cement will look somewhat rough once painted, so you may have to put up a wall to hide it.

Poured cement foundations are best for deep basements or where strength is an important issue. You should consider poured foundations if the site is undeveloped and having cement trucks pull up isn't going to damage the property. You will pay more for poured foundations, so for most additions, they are probably not necessary.

Make sure that rebar (half-inch metal reinforcing rods) is installed in the foundation before pouring, and ask whether the strength of the concrete is in line with your local building codes.

Walls

Typically, walls are made of wood or steel studs with plasterboard screwed or nailed onto them.

- Wood studs are standard for residential work in most of the country. Since they are made of wood, they tend to shrink, expand, and warp. They require a fair bit of force to cut or drill through as opposed to steel studs. They also burn. They are strong, readily available, and carpenters like to work with them.

- Steel studs are standard in commercial work. They are made of thin-gauge steel with holes punched through them at regular intervals. They tend to be flimsy until plasterboard has been attached to them and may be slightly more expensive and more difficult to get than wood studs. They are consistently straight, are not affected by atmospheric conditions, are lightweight and easy to cut with a pair of tin cutters. They also don't burn, so when used with Sheetrock, they provide fireproof walls.

■ Plasterboard—or Sheetrock, which is the most widely known brand—is reinforced-plaster sandwiched between two sheets of paper that come in standard sizes. Plasterboard doesn't stop sound very well, sounds hollow when you knock on it, and if done clumsily, the joints between the boards are obvious. It's very fast, economical, and relatively easy to use, provides a flat wall surface, and is the industry standard.

Make sure that the contractor insulates your Sheetrock, even in interior walls, which will improve the sound transmission problem. Also watch that he uses screws instead of nails, even for wood. (When wood studs warp, they will pull away from the Sheetrock, pulling the nails out of the wood as they go. When humidity changes and the studs warp back, these nails will be pushed out through the face of the Sheetrock.) Watch that the person who finishes the plasterboard with compound is a professional taper. A good taper makes all the difference.

To make your Sheetrock walls look more smooth, you can have new Sheetrock work completely skimmed with joint compound. Rather than just taping the joints and covering the nail holes, savvy clients may choose to have the whole wall thinly coated with joint compound.

To make the walls look even more smooth, some contractors skim the walls with plaster instead of compound. Plaster is great and nothing is better for skimming walls; but once you prime and paint the walls, there will be little notable difference between plaster and joint compound.

- Plaster walls are very rare these days. They are strong, fire-resistant (plaster gives off trapped water molecules when heated), and slightly bumpy. It is difficult to find anyone to make them anymore. They are also messy and expensive to make.

Flooring

Attached to the flooring joists (or frames for the floor) is a "sub-floor" which is often plywood or chipboard. In older houses the sub-floor is usually strips of soft wood. This subfloor can be covered with a variety of materials.

- Solid hardwood strip floor is generally made from 3/4-inch-thick by 2½-inch-wide strips of solid wood (oak or maple usually but also cherry and other hardwoods) laid side by side and nailed to the subfloor. Depending on the kind of wood used, it is relatively expensive, requires professional installation, and is prone to squeaks. However, this kind of floor will finish beautifully and can be sanded many times, making it unlikely that it will ever need replacement. Make sure that the wood is what you ordered and that it is of good quality—and that when it is installed, the joints are tight.

- Solid parquet floor is made of ½-inch-thick by 3/4-inch-wide strips of hardwood glued down in tiles. They are relatively expensive, the glue can fail from age or water, and tiles can become loose (though they are easy enough to glue back down). They will finish beautifully and can be sanded many times as well, though not often as a strip floor.

For wood floors, you have the following finish choices:

- Polyurethane is the standard. Polyurethane is a natural product of various resins, but when it was originally introduced, it was given an artificial-sounding name to make it more "scientific." Glossy polyurethane can look plastic and cheap, but whatever the finish, polyurethane is strong, scratch-resistant, and relatively stain-resistant. When applied in a matte finish, it can look quite nice.

Over the years, the EPA has been cracking down on oil-based products to cut down on air and water pollution. This has brought about the introduction of water-based polyurethane.

- Oil-based polyurethane takes a day to dry, gives off fumes while drying, and is prone to yellow with age. Positively, it is strong and resistant to staining from spills and water.

- Water-based polyurethane isn't as impervious to water, but it doesn't yellow. It dries very fast and without fumes and is very strong as well. I highly recommend it for occupied homes. I like it for unoccupied homes as well, and it is certainly better for the environment. Soon, it may be the only choice, as oil-based products are gradually banned from the marketplace.

- Rubbed oil finishes are rare, and for good reason. The floor has to be perfectly smooth for this finish to look good. Rubbed oil floors are more prone to stain than polyurethane floors. They also must be periodically rewaxed and often re-oiled. Positively, maintenance doesn't require the sanding off of the finish that a polyurethane does; another coat of oil is all that's usually needed. The floor can look very natural and pretty. Because of emission standards, though, oils won't be around much longer.

No matter the finish, make sure that the floor is sanded very smoothly with no marks from the sanding machine. This will determine the quality of the finished floor.

- Laminated parquet floors are made from a veneer of hardwood glued to another less expensive wood and are generally sold in tiles one foot square by a half inch thick. The veneer on these floors is thin, so you can't really sand it down to refinish it. The floor will buckle if it gets wet enough and is prone to glue failure, causing squeaks. It's not a very good choice for the long run. Positively, it comes prefinished so it is economical to install and can be relatively attractive.

Other than wood, you can cover your subfloors with a number of other materials:

- Nylon carpets are the standard. Many emit noxious formaldehyde fumes when first installed and build up static electricity. Positively, they wear well, are stain-resistant, inexpensive, and come in a wide variety of styles and weaves.

- Wool carpet is expensive and may not yield much return on resale, because the new owners may want to redecorate. Positively, it cleans well, wears very well, and is beautiful.

- Ceramic tile requires professional installation, a firm subfloor, and a good design if you're using more than one color. If the installation isn't very good, the tiles tend to crack, so be sure to stockpile some extra tile in case of breakage in the future. Ceramic tile is relatively expensive, but it is beautiful, will last forever, and cleans up very well.

- Stone, marble, or granite requires skilled craftsmen to install, a very firm subfloor, and an installation method that ensures that the stone doesn't crack. Installation also requires an artistic eye and a willingness to discard at least 20 percent of the stone to achieve a nice-looking pattern. White marble stains (though a mixture of plaster of paris made with bleach rather than water will remove most stains). Most other stones will not stain. They are slippery, though a "honed" finish makes them less slippery. Stone is expensive, but it lasts forever, adds resale value if done well, and looks beautiful. It makes for lovely entrance hall, bathroom, and kitchen floors because it is relatively impervious to moisture and dirt. It is real and has real beauty.

Windows

A window's performance is judged not only by its aesthetics and mechanical reliability but also by its ability to seal and keep out dirt, water, sound, and temperature variations. Windows should also be judged by their expected longevity.

- Vinyl windows are made of vinyl frames and insulated glass. Because they are vinyl, they are affected by exposure to the sun, specifically ultraviolet light. Remember the vinyl roofs once popular on cars? They looked great for the first year or two but soon they became cracked and stained. Likewise, vinyl windows may discolor, become brittle, and eventually break. They can't easily be painted because the paint won't adhere well to the frame. Positively, they are the least expensive, and at least at the beginning, they work well mechanically. Aesthetically, vinyl windows can be molded to resemble a wood window frame so they are attractive. If the rest of the house isn't worth much, vinyl windows are a reasonable alternative. Manufacturers are claiming improvements in the process and now offer longer warrantees.

- Wood windows are made from soft wood and insulated glass. At one time, the insulating value of glass wasn't so important because people installed storm windows in the winter. When insulating glass came into existence, storm windows weren't needed, but a better method of cutting down on the draft between sash and track was. Wood windows often use a vinyl track, and like all vinyl, it can break down in UV light, becoming brittle and cracked. Wood windows are somewhat limited in strength and can't hold as thick or as large a piece of insulated glass as an aluminum window. Because they are wood, they require either paint or polyurethane. They are the most attractive of the windows, they can be painted to match the interior and exterior trim, and they usually function well mechanically.

Some manufacturers now cover the outside wood with either aluminum or an epoxy-painted finish. Because wood windows expand and contract with changes in temperature and humidity, the aluminum can split apart from the wood.

Solid wood windows made by one of the big manufacturers are lovely. They're relatively expensive but offer solid resale value because they'll still work well mechanically and look good ten years from now.

- Aluminum windows are made from pressed aluminum frames with rubber materials. Aluminum basically comes out in flat forms, so the curves and volume of a wood window are impossible with an aluminum one. The choice of colors will also be limited to white, black, bronze, and maybe a few others. They are the most expensive and probably the least attractive. They are mechanically the best, though. They will seal out the elements forever, and with a baked enamel finish they'll probably never need maintenance and can look like new for a long time.

The bigger manufacturers are now producing better-looking windows.

Cabinets

The main differences between cabinets depend on who has made them and what materials they are made of. Cabinets are judged by their aesthetics, their functional practicality and use of space, the quality of their mechanical function, and finally by their resistance to wear and tear.

- Site-built cabinets are used by a contractor trying to save the client money and make himself a little in the bargain. They may be rough-looking, but because they are custom-made, they will maximize space. They probably won't function mechanically very well or resist abuse.

- Low-end mass-produced cabinets are almost all white, or beige with oak trim. They look neutral and won't maximize space because they are only sold in certain dimensions. They will function mechanically for a while but won't stand up well to day-to-day abuse.

- Well-made, contractor-assembled cabinets will be built by the contractor on-site from pieces he's had cut or manufactured. These cabinets can be relatively attractive, as there are many producers of quality door and drawer fronts. They'll likely maximize space because they'll be designed to fit your space. They'll function well mechanically because the contractor will probably use high-quality hardware—though they'll lack the hi-tech items of high-end commercial cabinets. They will be relatively resistant to abuse, although their finish may not be as smooth or strong as a high-end commercial cabinet.

- High-end commercial cabinets are manufactured to custom specifications in the United States or stock specifications in Europe. Aesthetically, they will be very nice, and they will use the space fairly well because of the wide range of sizes. They function well mechanically, with nice hi-tech items like spice racks, mixer lifts, and lazy Susans. They are relatively resistant to abuse.

- Cabinetmaker cabinets are manufactured by a local cabinet shop. Aesthetically, they can be very good, with complete flexibility in material and finish. These cabinets maximize the use of the space and function well mechanically, with many of the high-tech items of the high-end commercial cabinets. They are very resistant to abuse and can be repaired at a later date.

Countertops

- Plastic laminate (Formica is the common brand) is the most popular countertop. Formica is made of two pieces bonded together: a high-pressure plastic top surface and a black "substrate" on the bottom. Looking at a piece of Formica from above, you don't see the black substrate, but when two sheets fit together at right angles (like the front edge of a countertop), the edge of the Formica is revealed and you can see the black substrate. Many consider this aesthetically unappealing. To avoid this, investigate the more expensive versions of plastic laminate in which the color is consistent throughout the material, without a black substrate. This black edge can also be covered by a solid wood or metal edge piece which also protects the edge from chipping, Formica's biggest problem. Formica is also easily burned by cigarettes or hot pans, and scraped by knives. The surface can bubble up and delaminate with time—especially the varieties without the substrate.

  Plastic laminate is stain-resistant, easy to clean up, relatively easy to fabricate, comes in hundreds of colors, and takes very little time to fabricate, as most contractors cut counters themselves.

- Stainless steel doesn't fit in very well with "pretty" kitchens and requires a specialized fabricator who may not be local. Stainless steel can also dent. Otherwise, it is impervious to water, will look new even after thermonuclear war.

- Butcher-block counters stain when used around the sink, as water invariably leaches into the wood and generates black mold. To counteract that, many use a different material next to the sink. By its nature, butcher block will get banged up, require regular lemon-oil maintenance, and will never be as hygienic as other materials. It will also burn, although any damage can be sanded out. It is relatively easy to fabricate, relatively inexpensive, and some believe it gets better looking through use. Maple is stronger than oak but oak still works well.

- Marble is relatively soft and porous, particularly white marble. It can be scratched and pitted and requires skilled fabricators and installers. Because marble is difficult to trim at the job site, exact measurement "templates" are made to the dimensions of the installed cabinets. The whole process can take a few weeks. Marble derives its beauty from its organic patterns, and each slab is different from another. It's therefore important to choose the slab you want and even where in the slab your countertops should be cut from. Otherwise, marble is beautiful, has a cool working surface, which is good for making pastry, and adds solid resale value. Marble comes in a wide variety of colors and textures.

- Granite requires even more competent workmanship than marble does because while marble is softer and can be smoothed and polished on the job site, granite is very hard and needs to be perfect the first time. Because each piece of granite is different, it's important to pick out the exact slab you want and perhaps even where in the slab you want your countertops cut from. Granite is less variable than marble, though, and many varieties of granite are extremely consistent. It also comes in fewer attractive varieties than marble. Otherwise, it is the premier countertop material. It is hard, nonporous, scratch-resistant, and like stainless steel, will survive most wars.

■ Slate must be of high quality or it will stain. Slate is also softer than granite, so it can chip. It has a beautiful soft black appearance, and high-quality slate is very good for countertops. It's fairly expensive.

■ A "solid surface" material like Corian is a thick piece of hard plastic which, like granite or marble, serves as the counter but does not need any kind of wood backing the way plastic laminates do. It is as expensive as granite (where granite is readily available) but is not as beautiful as solid stone in my opinion. However, it has many advantages. It can be fused together so that sinks, countertops, and backsplashes can flow together without any seams. This means that it can be kept extremely clean. It can take a great deal of abuse—burns, cuts, dings—and be sanded out by the owner to a like-new condition. It comes in many colors which are consistent with samples. Corian only sells its material to certified fabricators, so you'll have to find them in your area, but someone will likely cover your hometown. It's a very nice material that will add to your resale value and is second in appearance only to stone.

■ Ceramic tile countertops can crack, especially if poorly installed, but tiles can always be replaced if you've bought enough extras. I'd recommend buying a good twenty extra tiles just in case. Glazed tile is stain-resistant though the grout is not (a sealer will counteract this). Tile countertops vary widely in price, depending on the price of the tiles. They can look quite attractive, they are easy to fabricate, and the only lead time is waiting for the tile to arrive.

Lighting Fixtures

Light varies in the quality and quantity of light, the visibility of the fixture, the cost, and the hum. Lights having the "UL" label (which means they've been tested and approved by the insurance industry's watchdog: Underwriters' Laboratories) will have safe mechanical and electrical construction. You must demand this. There are cheap imports which lack the label and have been known to set fire to houses every year. Design quality is something to be decided with your design professional.

- Recessed lights are mounted in the ceiling. Their position is permanent, and they provide some eye glare since the bulb is exposed. Because their light shoots straight down, the light produces strong shadows unless there are many of them. They are not appropriate in traditional interiors.

- Track lights sit on tracks on the ceiling. The position and direction of the lights can be adjusted, so they are excellent for illuminating rows of pictures or cabinets.

  Track lighting fixtures using standard incandescent bulbs are usually large and often appear ungainly. They have a habit of changing styles every few years, leaving most track lighting systems looking dated.

  Tracks using quartz-halogen fixtures are much more minimal, have a whiter light, are more expensive, and may not look dated for some time. Quartz-halogen bulbs usually require a transformer, which will be the size of a children's shoe box and fit tucked in a hole somewhere. In some cases each fixture will have its own transformer. When dimmed, these transformers, the dimmers, or the fixtures themselves can hum like a hive of bees.

- Surface-mounted lights are traditional, and depending on their design, may use some kind of shading device to produce fewer shadows and draw attention to themselves. They are good at providing general room light but not adjustable lighting.

- Undercabinet lighting provides task lighting without being obvious. There are incandescent bulbs that cast a yellow light, fluorescent bulbs that make a blue-white light, and halogen bulbs that make a bright white light. The negative quality (harsh, vibrating light) of fluorescent bulbs isn't nearly as bad when placed undercabinet because the light bounces off the countertops, diffusing it before it strikes the eye.

Plumbing Fixtures

Plumbing codes regulate plumbing fixtures because public health relies on it. So, unless you buy your plumbing fixtures in another country, they should be safe. They may not, however, be effective.

- Toilets are being redesigned to use less water. Older toilets often use 3.5 gallons of water per flush, while new toilets use 1.6 gallons. While the older toilets are certainly wasteful, many newer toilets don't do a very good job of keeping the bowl clean and taking all of the waste out in one flush. Few showrooms have toilets set up for demonstrations, so the best you can do is get a recommendation from the plumber, architect, or contractor for a specific toilet, then ask to speak with a client who has one of those toilets installed. All you have to do is ask what they think of that brand of toilet. They may not come right out and say it, but if they don't like their toilet, you'll know. This matter is important because so many of the new, low-flow toilets don't do a good job and it is frustrating when you use it every day.

- Faucets

    Old-style faucets use a rubber washer and a seat arrangement that requires your pressure to stop the flow of water. New faucets use a ceramic valve that relies on close engineering tolerances instead. These are far superior.

    Brass, by its nature, tarnishes; therefore, a coating must

be used to keep the lacquer from tarnishing. If that lacquer is scratched, tarnish can set in, so you must be extremely careful cleaning and maintaining brass bathroom fixtures. Chrome-plated brass fixtures are much more durable, as are stainless steel fixtures.

■ Tubs

Tubs are made of three different materials: (1) sheet metal coated with enamel, which is tinny-sounding, inexpensive, and adds little value to a house but will save the plumber's back on installation; (2) some form of plastic, which has a better sound, isn't cold to the touch, can be scratched with abrasive cleansers, and will save the plumber's back on installation; (3) cast iron with a porcelain surface, which has a beautiful sound, retains the heat of the water, can't be scratched easily, and will have your plumber cursing you to his chiropractor.

Negotiation

I began thinking about writing this book when Joe Kocy, a state planner and my brother-in-law, gave me a copy of *Getting to Yes,* by Robert Fisher and William Ury. *Getting to Yes* is a short summation of the Program on Negotiation at Harvard Law School, and it answered precisely the questions I'd had about how to negotiate well without developing a bad reputation. Reading the book led me to Boston for a semester at the Program on Negotiation, which led me to write the papers that this book is based on.

If you want to learn how to negotiate well, I highly recommend that you read *Getting to Yes.* Additionally, Christopher W. Moore's *The Mediation Process* has been invaluable.

From these two books and my own experiences, I have learned what the key steps are to good negotiation.

Look to satisfy your needs and the needs of those around you. Often, we imagine that our needs and the needs of those we are bargaining against are mutually exclusive: *If I get what I want, you can't get what you want—there's simply not enough in the pot.* Or perhaps we believe that the other side doesn't matter, that we only need to concentrate on getting what we want in order to win.

The key to good negotiating is not manipulation, but identification of your own needs and the needs of the side you are negotiating with. The goal is then to satisfy as many of those needs for each other as you possibly can. A negotiated agreement based on these goals will produce a wise, efficient solution that doesn't need as much enforcement because it's good for both sides.

It's my experience that almost all problems have simple solutions; it's just a matter of jumping the hurdles that are in our way to finding them. We lack faith that a mutually beneficial solution exists, and we act selfishly and forcefully in the hope that we can have our way by demanding it.

We also allow emotions to interfere with objective appraisal of the situation. Fears and emotions don't do well suppressed, so I'm not advocating that we squash our feelings. Rather, we must establish a simple strategy for acknowledging them and moving past them. The easiest way to do this is to identify the fear and communicate it. *"Mary, this makes me very nervous to spend this much money for a bathroom." "Bill, it makes me angry that you said you were starting yesterday and you didn't show up." "Tom, it would make me feel very vulnerable if I were to give you half the money for the project before you started."*

Everyone involved in home renovation and construction will not have had the opportunity to read this book or *Getting to Yes*. You, on the other hand, have read it, so you're going to have to help the others express their feelings. *"Tom, I imagine it angers you that I'm not willing to give you a down payment today." "Fran, I imagine it's frustrating that I'm rejecting this plan."*

This may feel odd to you (see, I'm doing it to you now) but it works consistently. For some reason people don't like to admit that they are angry, but if you say it for them, I have found that most people are very willing to agree. A psychologist might say it's because you are making it legitimate for them to feel this way.

By using this strategy you are not agreeing that you've done wrong but you are seeing things from their point of view. Additionally, by restating their complaint, you have made what Fisher and Ury call the Cheapest Concession. You have let them know that they are heard. You are not agreeing with them, but you have listened to them so that now they can return the favor and listen to you. Having heard each other, you can begin to negotiate a solution.

In the case of construction, I believe each of the participants' needs are centered around a beautiful project, on time and on budget. Such a project would be good for the client, contractor, and architect. However, on further investigation, you may find needs that are unique to each participant. Perhaps the owners have a specific amount of money they can afford to spend. Perhaps the contractor has a large-scale job starting in six weeks and needs to finish this project before then. Perhaps the architect has been offered a magazine pictorial on her next project and she wants to concentrate on that. These needs must be sought out and understood by all the participants.

The next step to effective negotiation is to generate multiple options for resolution of all these needs. Say, for instance, that we are looking to negotiate a final price. The contractor wants to have adequate money to do first-quality work and he wants to be compensated for his time. The owners' budget is somewhat flexible. They want the best-quality work but they don't want to spend more than they have to. The architect wants this negotiation to go well because she likes the contractor and the client, and needs recommendations from the client. They all want a beautiful project. So, options for them might be:

1. Contractor does all work for $16,000 (making owner happy).

2. Contractor does all work for $30,000 (making contractor happy).

3. Contractor does work for $20,000 but substitutes less expensive cabinets (contractor and owner fairly happy; architect a little less happy).

4. Contractor does all work for $26,000 but installs a ceramic instead of a vinyl floor in the kitchen, uses less expensive cabinets in an excellent line, and agrees to a full professional cleaning service during the job. (All three end up happy with this solution.)

Depending on the negotiation, you may want to use "objective criteria" to examine the validity of the deal. For instance, if you adjust the work to what the contractor says he can do for $45,000, you then need to ask other contractors to look at the same work and find out what their prices are. If two other qualified contractors quote prices in the $30,000 range, you might come to the conclusion that your original contractor is too expensive. On the other hand, finding that other contractors will charge you nearly the same or more may put you at ease with the contractor you would like to work with.

Using objective criteria is a good way to deal with negotiation deadlock. Say the contractor wants $300 for the medicine cabinet. You think the price is ludicrous and only want to pay $100. Nobody wants to back down because neither solution saves face for the loser. Instead, the contractor should offer to check prices for ready-made medicine cabinets, and the owner should check the prices of other contractors' bids. By doing this, the answer will make itself clear.

If you are patient in following these general guidelines, a solution will surface or more options will be generated.

This is a brief discussion of negotiation strategy and truly an inadequate shortcut. If you can, read *Getting to Yes*.

Contracts

The standard contract used in the professional renovation market is the American Institute of Architects (AIA) Form A107, Abbreviated Form of Agreement Between Owner and Contractor for Construction Projects of Limited Scope Where the Basis of Payment Is a Stipulated Sum, 1987 edition. This document is used because it is reasonably fair to all parties, carefully covers the problems and responsibilities of construction, and has been tested extensively in the courts. Often, contractors will offer their own contracts which set forth the work to be done and the amount to be paid. These documents become useless, though, when problems occur. The AIA document sets in writing terms for termination, rates of interest for late payment, means of dispute resolution, and many other concerns for owners. The wide-ranging nature of the document protects both owner and contractor and saves legal bills later on by making the terms of the agreement explicit.

For works of larger scope, the AIA suggests A101 with its supplementary condition form A201. The rule of thumb is that projects over $150,000 use the A101. I'll include my comments for A107 first, then A101.

The AIA also produces a document for projects that are based on a cost-plus method. In a cost-plus scenario, the contractor is paid for his time and materials at an agreed-upon rate plus a fee. This arrangement doesn't require the contractor to commit to the cost of the project ahead of time. Instead, the contractor will charge the owner exactly what it costs him to build the project (materials and wages) plus an agreed-upon fee or percentage of the overall cost for the contractor. This may seem like a great idea, but in this plan, there is little incentive for the contractor to work efficiently and quickly because the longer it takes him and the higher the bills add up, the more the contractor will make. This method also makes it very difficult to budget the project since there is no set budget.

The reason time and materials should be included in the budget is because the project is too difficult for the contractor to bid accurately. The contractor will budget more money and time for those things that are not specified in the budget.

The cost-plus method can work, but only if it relies on the ethics of the contractor, or on some kind of bonus for the contractor if he saves the client money over the other bids.

It is my opinion that you should not be entering into a project with a contractor who finds the plans too difficult to bid on—how is he expecting to actually perform the work? If all the contractors bidding on the project are high, then you have to guess that maybe they are all right and it's the architect who's underestimating the difficulty of the work.

Asking for bids for time and material without a finished plan is pure folly. I recognize that there are situations in which it seems prudent to start design and construction at the same time. But experience shows, if you took two projects, one that started immediately and one that had to wait for a completed design, both would finish at nearly the same time. Designing as you go creates mistakes that will have to be redone. Say you have a limited time to construct a foyer that leads into a dining room. You design the foyer, start building it, then start to design the dining room. Once you do, though, you realize that the opening into the dining room is centered on the foyer side but markedly off center on the dining room side. So you have to stop work on the foyer while you change the centerline. Electrical wiring must be moved, cabinets cut down or abandoned, flooring changed— all at a high, change-order cost. Even though you might have had to wait two weeks to get complete plans, it will take at least that long to correct your work.

I think the reason the cost-plus bid is suggested is that the architect doesn't want to admit that she hasn't taken the time to finish the plans and instead suggests that this will be easier. In the long run it's not. The easiest way to maintain control of your project is to make sure you meet all design deadlines for plans and bids.

You should also require that your contractor make proper contracts between himself and his subcontractors. I recommend AIA form A401. This assures that if there is a problem with the subcontractor, you and your contractor will be protected. Contractors often don't write contracts with their subcontractors because they've known each other for so long that they have complete trust in each other. They've agreed to a price and the amount of work. What more is there? For them, contracts seem only to sow seeds of suspicion.

But when unexpected trouble occurs (pipes break, fires start, people are injured), these documents will assure proper distribution of liability. If you require executed copies of contractor/subcontractor contracts, it gives the contractor an excuse to protect himself. Don't ask to see the price of the contracts, though.

Following are some notes and instructions to keep in mind when using the AIA A107 contract.

Page 1 Obvious.

Page 2, 1.1 In this section you should list those things that aren't included in contractor's work but aren't specified as such in blueprints to be NIC (not in contract).

2.1 List the start date.

2.2 List date of completion and then something like this in second section:

> *Contractor will be paid $25 a day if he finishes before this date including punchlist. Owner will be paid $25 a day if he finishes after this date including punchlist. Saturdays and Sundays do not count. Change orders will include adjustments to time.*

3.1 Obvious.

3.2 Include the prices of doing things alternate ways. As much as possible, you should make up your mind before signing the contract, but in some instances that's impossible—for instance, until you break ground, you may not know the depth of the water table. By defining in the contract the cost per foot of digging, you can't be held hostage later by a contractor who's already started.

You may also be wavering over the floor in the kitchen. In 3.2 you would list the price for doing a vinyl floor instead of ceramic.

3.3 Here you should indicate the hourly wage of change orders as well as the percentage fee on materials. For instance:

> *For changes in which a lump sum is not agreed to, the rate will be mechanics $25/hour, assistants $15/hour, and a 15% fee will be charged on top of all materials. A written authorization by the owner is essential before commencement of the work. Beginning the work without such authorization ends the obligation of the owner to pay for such work.*

That's a stiff warning, but it assures that you will get change orders and that at the end of the job the contractor doesn't think of you as having deep pockets.

Here you could also list unit prices for items that aren't yet decided. You may know you have some rotting joists but you don't know how many. You could write in:

> *Joists to be replaced for $75/joist. No joists included in contract at present.*

4.1 Should read "See attached Pay Schedule."

Sample Pay Schedule

Payment schedule for Hampton Residence, 19 East Parkchester, Middlepath, N.Y.

Total job: $60,000

Down payment: 10%, or $6,000

Leaving $54,000, which will divide into 6 payments of $9,000

The payments then proceed as follows:

Each time Rusk Renovation completes $10,000 worth of work ($\frac{1}{6}$ of the job) a payment of $9,000 is made ($\frac{1}{6}$ of the money left to be paid after the down payment is deducted).

Payment 1 at $10,000	**$9000**
Payment 2 at $20,000	**$9000**
Payment 3 at $30,000	**$9000**
Payment 4 at $40,000	**$9000**
Payment 5 at $50,000	**$9000**
Payment 6 at $60,000 and satisfaction of punchlist	**$9000**

Extras and changes are 50% down, 50% on completion.

The contractor will give the owner two days' advance warning before submitting a pay request. The owner will have two days to approve the pay request and then wire the money into contractor's account. Pay requests may be for more than one unit.

Wire payments to:

Rusk Renovation
Account #00000000
ABA #00000000
Bank branch #000
223 Fairbank Street
Anytown, USA

6.1.2 Should include Pay Schedule.

6.1.3 List the specifications according to the "Solutions to Quality Problems" from the "Contracting Phase" section of this book. You should also list the job breakdown the contractor supplied, which will be used to determine the value of the work completed for the Pay Schedule.

6.1.4 Obvious.

6.1.5 There probably won't be addenda.

6.1.6 There probably won't be other documents not already listed.

In article 10, section 10.8, you should write in after "All claims or disputes between the contractor and the owner arising out or relating to the Contract, or the breach thereof, shall"

> *first be submitted to the following neutral mediator [name of mediator] and the parties shall attempt to resolve the dispute through mediation. Failing that, the dispute shall . . .*

This provides a ready and accessible means to resolve most disputes. The nonprofit institute I've founded, the American Renovation Association (ARA), will eventually offer a 900 pay-per-call number with instant mediation over the phone line to our members. You can also call the American Arbitration Association in your hometown and have one of their mediators assigned to your project. You should name a mediator in your contract. It's a lot easier to have someone in place than to try to agree on someone in the middle of an argument.

The rest of the contract to my mind is fine. Remember, I am not a lawyer, so I advise you to have your lawyer examine this document before you sign it.

Following are notes concerning the A101 contract. (Don't bother with this if you are using the A107.)

Page 1 Obvious.

Page 2, 3.2 List the date of completion.

3.3 List date of completion. Refer to my notes for section 2.2 of the A107 contract.

4.2 Refer to my notes for section 3.2 of the A107 contract.

4.3 Refer to my notes for section 3.3 of the A107 contract.

5.2 Should read "See attached Pay Schedule." Use sample pay schedule in A107 instructions.

5.3 to 5.8 Cross out.

9.1.3 May be blank.

9.1.4 List the specifications according to "Solutions to Quality Problems" in the "Contracting Phase" section of this book.

9.1.7 List the contractor's broken-down bid, which will be used with the payment request to determine payments.

In article XXX, section XXXX of AIA A201, General Conditions for A101, you should write in after "All claims or disputes between the contractor and the owner arising out or relating to the Contract, or the breach thereof, shall"

> *first be submitted to the following neutral mediator [name of mediator] and the parties shall attempt to resolve the dispute through mediation. Failing that, the dispute shall . . .*

See additional notes for section 10.8 of the A107 contract.

The rest of the contract in my mind is fine. Remember, I am not a lawyer, so I advise you to have your lawyer examine this document before you sign it.

Contracts can be ordered directly from the AIA at 1-800-365-2724. It is against the law to use photocopies of their contracts. You can also write to them at:

American Institute of Architects
Publication Department
1735 New York Ave. NW
Washington, DC 20006

Sample Change Order

We agree to make the following change:

Increase or decrease in job cost	_____
Increase or decrease in time to job completion	_____
Original job cost	_____
Net amount	_____
This change	_____
Total amount of change	_____
Total current job cost	_____
Original completion date	_____
Completion date after previous change orders	_____
New completion date	_____

Communication

Contractors constantly complain about the inability of the owner and architect to make decisions in a timely fashion. To solve this problem, contractors can't tell the client to "decide faster" and expect the situation to improve. The reason clients don't make decisions is that they lack the information needed to make the decision.

If the contractor's question is "What kind of countertops do you want?" the answer will be delayed until the owner knows the following: what types of countertop are available, what they look like, how they perform, how long they take to fabricate and install, and how much they cost.

This is quite a lot of information for the owner to receive and assimilate. So it is essential that the owner get this information as quickly as possible and in as clear a form as possible.

This process of amassing information is a vital part of every decision made during the project, from whether to write a check for a pay request to what color the walls in the bathroom should be painted. Accurate information is needed in order to move a project forward. Depending on how this information system is set up, decisions will be made wisely and efficiently, or slowly and agonizingly (and often incorrectly, causing changes later on).

I suggest the following:

- A fax machine is essential for the owner, architect, contractor, and "job site." It is a prerequisite of a smoothly functioning job. A fax speeds around requests for payments, change-order requests, and design sketches.

- Samples of paint colors, fabric, tile, marble, hardwood floor colors, etc., should have been decided well in advance, but in the real world, they are often not decided until the last minute. Often, these last-minute decisions drag past the last minute as samples are shipped back and forth. Be willing to use an overnight service to speed this communication in cases where the owner is not living at or near the home. In the case where the owner is living at some distance, I also suggest that the owner set up a mailing account and distribute shipping labels to everyone. Then the architect and contractor won't be hesitant to rush something, since they're not paying for it.

- The client, architect, and contractor must be able to reach each other quickly—often within an hour. The contractor will have a beeper but the others probably won't, so when they're not in their offices, there must be a way to reach them. Establish regular times for phone calls at home or get a cellular phone. Many clients want to talk to the contractor in the evenings, but some contractors just want to be with their families. Knowing for certain that you can call a contractor at six in the morning but not after eight at night will put your mind at ease and save the contractor wear and tear at home.

- Get emergency telephone numbers for all subcontractors so that if the lights blow or a pipe breaks, you can quickly get to the person you need. Always try the contractor first.

- To make conversation easier, make sure the rooms in the plans are labeled and then use those names. Call the big bedroom the Master Bedroom every time; the small room, Chip's Room, if that's how it goes on the plan. Keep rooms consistent in name and it will make it easier on everyone.

- Make sure that revised plans supplant older plans. When changes are made to the plan, you should make sure that the architect makes new plans and hands them out and that old copies of the plans are taped up and put away someplace safe. Usually, there aren't enough copies of the new plans, so the electrician might not get his own copy. If he's still operating off the old blueprint, when the walls go up, his wiring will be in the wrong place. Request extra copies and make sure the subcontractors get their copies as well. This will save you money and time in the long run.

- Pay attention to inconsistencies. Often I've been in discussions and someone has said something in passing that didn't make sense. When I've had the brains to follow up on it, I've saved myself big headaches because I've discovered there has been a major miscommunication—from putting a kitchen on the wrong side of the house to staining a floor that was supposed to be left natural.

- Remember, if it's not in writing, it doesn't count. What you may think is a resolute decision may be considered by your contractor a passing suggestion that never got followed up on. Put things in writing, use "memos of understanding" outlining what changes or requests you are making. Usually, contractors want to keep the momentum of their day going and are hesitant to take time out to write a change order. They will also want to see how long the change takes to make before deciding whether to charge for it or not. It's also possible that you've communicated your desire to make a change to a job site manager rather than the head contractor, who does all of the pricing. It may take time for the contractor to get around to the site to see exactly what you want to do and return a price to you.

As a result, if you are dealing with the president of the company on the job site (a contractor-carpenter), I highly recommend getting a price for the change in advance. In cases where the owner won't be on-site any time soon (a contractor-in-the-office), it might be better to go with a prenegotiated time and materials arrangement so that the change can be done immediately and be billed out later at the agreed-on rate, and the work can continue.

Dispute Resolution

Despite everyone's best efforts, mistakes occur in even the most co-operative jobs. It might be that the kitchen is painted the wrong color or that the air-conditioning system is faulty. There are three simple solutions to every mistake:

1. The problem can be ignored. The kitchen is the wrong color but maybe it works just as well.

2. The contractor fixes it for free.

3. The owner pays to have it fixed.

Perhaps everyone will agree to one of these solutions, particularly if it's a small problem. However, for big or costly mistakes, everyone probably won't agree to one of these "winner take all" solutions. Some kind of examination of the facts must be done and some kind of settlement must be made. There are three main methods to resolving these kinds of disputes.

Lawsuits

In a lawsuit, parties hire lawyers to represent their interests before a judge who renders a binding decision based on the facts.

The advantages of a lawsuit are that it is final, it removes the disputants from personal interaction with each other, and it leaves the decision up to a neutral third party. It will also make one of the participants victorious.

The chief disadvantages of lawsuits are that they are expensive, both in money and in time. Someone will lose and could lose in a dramatic way, and the relationship of the disputants will end. Lawsuits are a poor way to resolve most problems in construction and should be avoided, unless you want to end the relationship.

Binding Arbitration

In an arbitration, parties hire lawyers to represent their interest before someone who has experience in that particular field. In the case of construction disputes, the arbitrator will likely be an architect or possibly a contractor. Using the facts of the case, the arbitrator will make a binding decision using his or her specialized knowledge of the field. This decision will not be made part of public record.

The advantages of arbitration are that it is speedier, private, and cheaper.

The disadvantages of arbitration are that the arbitrator can render a speedy bad decision based on prejudice, and there is no appeal process. The relationship between the participants will be destroyed, and because it is a third-party decision, it's possible for one side to lose dramatically. An arbitrator may have a bias or misunderstand the facts, rule incorrectly, and the parties have no way to appeal the decision. It is final.

Mediation

In a mediation, the disputing parties use a trained neutral to help them negotiate a mutually acceptable agreement. Though the mediator may interview the disputants on the facts, the mediator isn't going to render a decision himself or herself—and therefore the expensive process of ascertaining the facts isn't needed. The mediator instead works to find a solution based on the interests of the disputants and may bring into the negotiation things beyond money, such as recognition or warrantee, to find a mutually acceptable solution.

The advantages of mediation are that it helps the disputants to find their own solution to the problem and often brings the parties together during the process. Because the mediator doesn't have to be educated to all the facts of the dispute, it's possible for the mediation to occur soon after the problem occurs and be resolved within the day.

Because the negotiation isn't binding until a "deal memo" is signed by both parties, the decision isn't binding, and neither side can "lose" because they are always free to walk away from the mediation. As a result, the participants are forced to work in good faith to find a solution that is satisfactory to both sides or face a lawsuit or arbitration. It is also relatively low-cost.

The disadvantages of mediation are that parties must meet face-to-face—or at least through a shuttle diplomat—and must confront their problems rather than relying on someone else to solve them. Because mediated solutions must be mutually acceptable, vengeance isn't possible.

Contractors who find themselves not getting paid also have a low-cost recourse. They can file a mechanic's lien on the owner's property. A mechanic's lien asserts in a sworn statement that the owner owes money to the contractor which hasn't been paid. Until this lien is satisfied, mortgages can't be taken on the property and sales are difficult. The property can even be foreclosed on in order to satisfy the lien. For contractors who haven't been paid what is clearly owed them, liens work in a straightforward manner. For liens that relate to extras—especially extras without clearly executed change orders— liens serve more as a method to get the owner to the bargaining table. Contractors must be very careful to make no misstatements when filing liens, as serious legal consequences will result.

Acknowledgments

I wish to thank William Ury and Roger Fisher, both for their work at the Program on Negotiation at Harvard Law School and for their book, *Getting to Yes*. My book is an application of their theories. Thanks to Bruce Stedman, who was my instruction at the Program on Negotiation and who encouraged me to turn my analysis of the construction industry into a pamphlet for my clients. Thanks to Jean MacDonald of the Jean MacDonald Literary Agency, who called me to put molding in her living room and instead convinced me to turn my pamphlet into a book. Thanks to Stuart Krichevsky of the Stuart Krichevsky Literary Agency, who guided this book from my pamphlet into its present form. He has been a great friend, advisor, negotiator, and perfectionist. Thanks to Lori Lipsky, the head of Main Street Books at Doubleday, who made this book one of her first acquisitions and believed so strongly in what I am trying to do. Even more, thanks to her for her great kindness during the writing of this manuscript.

Thanks to Rob Robertson, my good friend and editor at Doubleday, who has refined, simplified, and vastly improved my manuscript, as well as serving as its unfailing champion. Thanks also to copy editor William Betts for his fine work and the typesetters who suffered the final changes to this manuscript. Thanks to Russell Gordon for a beautiful cover.

Thanks to my many good clients who've made me their partners over the years; in particular, David Guc, Ruth and Jerome Porush, Bill and Sarah Boehmler, William and Melinda vandenHeuvel, Phyllis and Bill Rosser, Miriam Vasicka, Steve and Maia Weiss, Patricia and Andrew Soussloff, Phil Kann and Virginia Maddock, Natalie and Jordan Stern, Dick Olsen, Alan Zwerin and Mike Avram. Thanks to the fine architects and designers I work with; in particular, Sinclair

Rankin, Alastair Standing, and Terry Atkin, who have commented on my manuscript and worked with me to make improvements. And thanks to Conrad McMillan, Jeff Lydon, and David Scher for giving me my start in this business. Thanks to Daniel Simonis, Phillip Walker, Jim Gialamas, Brian Doyle, Giroid Dolan, Chester Layman, Tom Hardy, Marlon Vargas, Bertie Carolan, Jerry McGovern, Noah Lamy, Peter Lennarts, Komuro, Israel, Hgai, Garth, Larry, David Klien, Susan, and all the others who've helped me pull off so many beautiful jobs. Thanks to Jeff Decker for advice and referrals in the materials sections.

Thanks to God and Monsignor Wallace Harris.

Thanks to my mom and dad, who built for me a foundation of love and compassion. Thanks to my brothers, Clem, Bob, and Duane, for their endless encouragement. And thanks to my brother-in-law, Joe Kocy, for giving me *Getting to Yes* and starting me on this road.

Thanks to my daughters, Lillian and Eve, who sat on my lap and never erased a thing; and who are, well, just the best.

Most of all, great thanks to my wife, Mary Kocy, for her love, support, and editing. She managed to find what I was trying to say and help me say it. To her, all my love.

John Rusk is the owner of Rusk Renovation, a high-end renovation company in New York City with clients up and down Park Avenue, East End Avenue, the Village, SoHo, the Upper West Side, and everywhere in between. His clients have been as varied as a homicide detective in Harlem, the past president of the Art Deco Society of America, a board member of Time Warner and the vice-president of International Paper. Rusk Renovation also serves as construction management and general contractor for medical facilities such as the recently opened Sterling Dialysis Associates in Brooklyn, New York.

He's also the owner of Lost Art Molding, a company specializing in crown molding.

Born and raised in Missoula, Montana, Rusk has a bachelor of fine arts from Carnegie-Mellon University, where he was a National Merit Scholar. He studied negotiation theory at the Program on Negotiation at Harvard Law School, where his papers on the construction industry formed the basis of this book. He taught a seminal version of this book at Parsons School of Design called "Construction in the Real World: Contracting for Designers."

He is also a professional mediator and member of the American Arbitration Association, lending his negotiation skills to disputes in the construction industry, and is a member of DART—the Construction Industry Dispute Avoidance and Resolution Task Force. He is also a member of Painters and Decorators of America.

He is a member of the Writer's Room and is currently working on a historical spy thriller.

John Rusk is happily married and the father of two girls, Lillian and Eve.

Dear Reader,

Thanks for buying *On Time and on Budget*. If these ideas make sense to you, I'd like to invite you to join the American Renovation Association, a group of homeowners, architects, contractors, designers, suppliers, and manufacturers dedicated to beautiful renovations achieved through a positive, cooperative partnership.

If you would like more information on the American Renovation Association, or would like to become a member, please fill out the form on the next page and send it to:

> The American Renovation Association
> 112 Madison Avenue, 3rd Floor
> New York, NY 10016-7424

> Or call (212) 689-3247 for more information

John Rusk
President, American Renovation Association

Name

_____

Name of Business (if applicable)

_____

Address

_____

City

_____

_____ I would like to become a member of the American Renovation Association. Please send me information on how to join.

_____ Please send me more information on the American Renovation Association.

Homeowners:
Have you renovated your home before? _____

Professional Members
What is your profession? _____
How long have you been practicing? _____

The American Renovation Association is not associated with Doubleday.